"Georgian has always been a car__ __ __ contagious joy and a global ambassador of the Gospel. His testimony will set you ablaze with fresh faith to experience the fullness of the abundant life that is in Jesus!"

Dr. Ché Ahn, founder and president, Harvest International Ministry; founding and senior pastor, Harvest Rock Church, Pasadena, California; international chancellor, Wagner University

"Joy is not a wish or a want. Joy is a weapon! Georgian personifies joy and has stewarded this ministry well to the Body of Christ at large. Joy has been Georgian's weapon to transform culture, and those who do not understand the fuel that joy provides in the long road ahead are in danger of selling their car to pay for their petrol. I highly recommend this read for those who do not wish to make that fatal error."

Tomi Arayomi, RIG Nation

"Georgian Banov is one of the most joyous people I know. His unique background and powerful Holy Spirit encounters have enabled him to walk in and share the joy of the Lord like none other that I know. He's a dear friend. We've been on several missions together, and he is always the same—extremely joyful in all circumstances. You will love this book."

John Arnott, Catch The Fire, Toronto

"Georgian and his wife have been two of our closest friends for over two decades, a constant gift to us through countless trials and celebrations. Their testimony of supernatural joy beyond every trouble in this world is something we have preached and witnessed all around the world. Be blessed by it!"

Heidi G. Baker, Ph.D., co-founder and executive chairman of the board, Iris Global

"There has never been a time when *Joy!* was needed more in the Body of Christ. Georgian beautifully displays this through his own life story, coupled with strong biblical teaching. I have personally witnessed Georgian bringing to disaster zones a joy that seemed like it was otherworldly, like it didn't belong among the devastation. It is because he lives out this message better than anyone I have been connected to. If you want to live with one of the richest tools God has for you, read this book and buy it for anyone who needs a dose!"

Shawn Bolz, author, *Translating God, Through the Eyes of Love, Keys to Heaven's Economy*; television and podcast host

"Joy can seem so elusive to so many who love Christ. But Georgian reveals in his life's story that joy can become the one constant when we realize whose it is, how much He loves us and where He resides. Drink deeply!"

Mark J. Chironna, bishop, Church On The Living Edge

"Georgian Banov is completely qualified to write this book! He is truly an 'apostle of joy' who, along with his precious wife, Winnie, and their team, has spread the joy of the Lord into some of the darkest places of the world. As you read this book, you will catch the joy of the Lord for sure. Get ready to be filled!"

Patricia King, author, minister, television host

"It has been my delight and privilege to first meet and then become a friend to one of the great modern treasures of God, rescued and utterly transformed by His grace and goodness. Escaping from his own nation already deeply hurt by an adapted ugly philosophy forcing on its sad people an inhumanly damaging control, Georgian's daring quest for freedom was finally found, not just in another country, but in Christ. It is high time we rediscover this most lovely and primary reason God made us all in the first place: joy! Go now with Georgian and Winnie to find what they both see as His game changer!"

Winkie Pratney, author and speaker

"Georgian Banov gives a masterful theological exposition of the ecstatic joy of being in God's presence and, more importantly, how to experience that joy. Get this book and learn how to have righteousness, peace and joy in the Holy Spirit every day."

Gordon Robertson, president,
Christian Broadcasting Network

"Talk about joy! What a wonderful gift this long-awaited book is to the Body of Christ! Georgian's journey will inspire, encourage and provoke you to find this same freedom and joy that has marked Geogian's life. The revelation that Georgian carries has the power to transform, and the incredible fruit that has come from Georgian and Winnie's life work is testimony of this. Jump in and inhale this book—it will refresh, inspire and delight you!"

Katherine Ruonala, senior leader, Glory City Church,
Brisbane, Queensland; author, Supernatural Freedom,
Speak Life and Life with the Holy Spirit

"The apostle Paul tells us, 'Let joy be your continual feast' (1 Thessalonians 5:16 TPT). And what a feast you are going to have as you read this book. From living in Europe to living in ecstasy, Georgian has a message from God for us. You will gleefully discover the secrets of joy on a brand-new level. This book will rock your world and leave you wanting more joy. I found delight in every page. Get ready to receive a God-given joy that is out of this world. And get an extra copy for someone you know that needs the gift of joy!"

Brian Simmons, The Passion Translation Project

"This book is packed with great revelation about the finished work of Christ. But that is not all—it also provides the capacity to reproduce inside of you what you are reading. That probably is the power of the testimony. Georgian takes you on his life journey, and while you experience his and Winnie's adventures, you are plunging into the practical application of the revelation. Amazing!"

Martin Spreer, pastor, Christus-Gemeinde
(Christ Church), Duisburg, Germany

"The infectious joy that surrounds Georgian Banov is always a game changer. When I am with him, I feel the shift to hope and life. His intense focus on the atmosphere of the Holy Spirit has been sustained for decades. His messages, his violin and now his book will fill you with the joy needed in these challenging days we live in. Get it, read it and soak in its words."

Steve Witt, founding pastor, Bethel Cleveland

JOY!

Joy!

God's
Secret Weapon
for
Every Believer

GEORGIAN BANOV

Chosen

a division of Baker Publishing Group
Minneapolis, Minnesota

© 2021 by Georgian Banov

Published by Chosen Books
11400 Hampshire Avenue South
Bloomington, Minnesota 55438
www.chosenbooks.com

Chosen Books is a division of
Baker Publishing Group, Grand Rapids, Michigan

Printed in the United States of America

Library of Congress Cataloging-in-Publication Data
Names: Banov, Georgian, author.
Title: Joy! : God's secret weapon for every believer / Georgian Banov.
Description: Minneapolis, Minnesota : Chosen, a Division of Baker Publishing Group, 2021.
Identifiers: LCCN 2020042986 | ISBN 9780800799779 (trade paperback) | ISBN 9780800762254 (casebound) | ISBN 9781493428427 (ebook)
Subjects: LCSH: Joy—Religious aspects—Christianity.
Classification: LCC BV4647.J68 B36 2021 | DDC 241/.4—dc23
LC record available at https://lccn.loc.gov/2020042986

Cover design by Darren Welch Design

Copyright information continued on page 174.

21 22 23 24 25 26 27   7 6 5 4 3 2 1

Dedicated to

Jesus my Savior, who for the joy set ahead endured the cross. Through unspeakable suffering, You rescued us from this present evil age and brought us into Your Kingdom.

My heavenly Father, who relentlessly pursues the prodigals. Thank You for the privilege of participating in the joy of Your harvest and homecoming celebrations.

The precious Holy Spirit, who keeps us and instructs us daily. Your supernatural currents of love and joy empower us to do what Jesus paid for.

My radiant bride and best friend, Winnie, lovingly called Cóco. I treasure your insatiable hunger for the Word and prophetic insights into the mysteries and bliss found in our marriage union with Christ. You are also the inspiration and force behind our ministry to the poorest of the poor.

Our beautiful miracle daughter, Yana, whose tender heart and compassion helped expand the scope of our extravagant love feasts among the nations.

My mother, who bravely raised me in the best way that she could as a single mom under very difficult circumstances, and my father, who gave me the gift of music. I cannot wait to see you both in heaven.

Contents

Foreword by Bill Johnson   13

Acknowledgments   17

1. Jesus Encounter   19

2. Friendship with God   39

3. Discovering God as Father   51

4. Jesus to the Core   67

5. Faith inside Christ   77

6. Performance-Free Grace   91

7. The Sanctified Heart   105

8. God's Party for You   121

9. Joy Is Not Dessert—It's a Weapon   135

10. Supernatural Joy and Justice   155

Foreword

ow! I love this book, this man and this message! I don't know many people who are as qualified to write a book called *Joy!* as Georgian Banov. The joy of the Lord truly is his strength. This book is rich in inspiration, but carries deep insights from the Scripture that we might grow in authentic grace. Welcome to *Joy!* Welcome to the journey of a lifetime.

The Bible gives us two very different responses to joy. When King David brought the Ark of the Covenant into Jerusalem, the Bible says he danced wildly before the Lord, worshiping Him with abandoned joy. Michal, his wife and Saul's daughter, watched him from the palace and was not impressed. But David let her know that his joy in the Lord would not be dampened by her disdain. And the Bible says she "had no child to the day of her death" (2 Samuel 6:23). She lost the capacity to be fruitful by despising a joyful response to God.

Isaiah depicts a very different relationship with joy. He writes, "Shout for joy, O barren one, you who have borne no child; break forth into joyful shouting and cry aloud" (Isaiah

54:1a NASB1995). We all have places in our lives that have been affected by barrenness, areas where we have yet to see fruitfulness. And this prophetic message tells us to "shout for joy . . . cry aloud."

The word *cry* actually means "to scream." This is not a scream of fear; it is a scream of anticipation. It is a deliberate, extreme expression of joy. We are commanded to shout for joy while our barrenness is staring us in the face. We are to shout with extreme celebration before the answer comes. Anticipatory joy isn't reasonable from a human perspective, but it is logical from God's perspective, as joy is the partner of great faith. It is common sense when our eyes are locked on the Promise Keeper, the One who never lies, the One who is no respecter of persons.

For when we enter into joy in this manner, the Bible promises that we will bear more fruit than the woman who never had trouble conceiving. "For the sons of the desolate one will be more numerous than the sons of the married woman. . . . Your descendants will possess nations and will resettle the desolate cities" (Isaiah 54:1b, 3). When we become one with the Lord, He brings fruitfulness to our area of greatest barrenness. And, because of that, we have every reason to rejoice.

We must not trust our emotions above the truth of Scripture. Equally dangerous is to have a purely intellectual connection to God's Word without an emotional involvement with His presence. Since the Kingdom of God is "righteousness and peace and joy" (Romans 14:17), two thirds of the Kingdom are felt realities. Michal rejected the Kingdom when she scorned joy. But the barren woman's feeling of joyful anticipation was evidence of her faith. And that faith brought forth fruitfulness that reverberated throughout the nations. The people who choose joy before their circumstances change become the ones who change their circumstances.

I've been with Georgian and Winnie in many countries around the world. They continually amaze me with their lifestyle of joy. I think of him as the "apostle of joy"! Once we were deep in the city of Jerusalem, far from the crowd of tourists, because the Banovs wanted to take several of us for an evening meal at a neighborhood-type restaurant where only the locals go. And of course, Georgian brought his violin, which was his custom for many of our outings. He got up in the restaurant and began to play his joyful music. A party broke out, including the chefs and other paid staff, who began to beat on the pots and pans as though they were drums. People laughed and danced about. It was extraordinary. I don't know of anyone else who would have done that. And I certainly don't know of anyone else who would have considered that normal. Georgian and Winnie did. Amazing, wonderful and liberating, it was also a little bit embarrassingly fun. But I obviously needed that.

Georgian is intentional about joy. He understands the value it holds in the Kingdom of God; as the Scriptures say, it was "for the joy set before Him [that Jesus] endured the cross" (Hebrews 12:2). To witness Georgian's playfulness, his freedom and his delight in the Lord and interpret it as frivolity or even just a personality trait would be an error. Joy, to the Lord, is anything but frivolous. C. S. Lewis said, "Joy is the serious business of Heaven." And, as you will read in these pages, the joy that Georgian carries is something for which he has fought. He knows, in an intimate and experiential way, the surpassing power of joy.

I encourage people everywhere to read this profound and very timely message. It's more than just a wonderful book, although it is that. Georgian and Winnie have taken ground so that we, as the Church, might benefit. Their breakthrough is our inheritance. And that inheritance is joy. Read their testimonies and stories so that you may receive one of the greatest gifts Jesus ever gave us: His *joy*.

Bill Johnson, Bethel Church, Redding, California;
author, *Born for Significance*, *The Way of Life*,
Raising Giant-Killers, *The Mind of God* and more

Acknowledgments

Many thanks to our Global Celebration partners and intercessors who have helped Winnie and me carry the life-transforming message of the cross to the nations, and who have helped us rescue and care for at-risk children on three continents. Together we are making a difference, and I believe you will personally hear Jesus say, "Insofar as you did it for the least of these, you did it for Me; well done!"

Thanks to my incredible Global Celebration team. I am privileged that you stand and believe with me, and I am grateful for your labor of love. It is a joy to serve the Lord together with all of you.

Thanks also to Karen Vangor, who helped me put this book together. Your editing and input were invaluable in helping me communicate my heart with clarity. I also want to thank Jane Campbell and David Sluka of Chosen Books for your excellence, patience and steady encouragement throughout this project.

1

Jesus Encounter

I was born and raised in Bulgaria under the stranglehold of Communism. The Communist party used fear and mind control to dominate us, and my own sense of personal identity was elusive. Emotionally, I felt dead inside. While the party elite had special privileges, the rest of us existed on rations. Meat and fresh vegetables were seldom seen in our stores—we were given just enough to keep the cogs in their machine turning: espresso coffee to wake us in the morning, bread to fill our bellies at daytime, and cheap vodka to numb us down at night.

I had fully resolved to escape, even if it meant I would die trying. Knowing that the Bulgarian KGB would eventually interrogate every one of my relatives and friends, I could not breathe a word about the escape to anyone. If they were to learn about my plans and not try to stop me or report me to the police, their lives would be made miserable. Those who resisted the Communists ended up in labor camps or, at the very least, faced serious civil restrictions and punishments.

My application for a travel visa had been submitted, and I was waiting for my paperwork to arrive. I was scheduled to play a gig with a band in one of the nightclubs in East Berlin, the Communist portion of Germany. From there I would have some mobility and could venture my escape through the Iron Curtain. As soon as my papers arrived, my plan would be put into motion.

Anxious thoughts and raging fears boiled inside of me. I could not sit still at home, so I would go out to take brisk walks. It was fall and cold outside. Pacing around the streets of Sofia with the chill of the air against my face helped me keep it together, somewhat.

During one of my walks, I headed down a side street where I found a door slightly ajar. I pushed it open to see what was inside. Immediately there was a whiff of warm air mixed with a scent I could not identify. I could see a long stairway leading underground, so I went inside to get warm and to investigate. At the bottom of the stairs there was a little spring of water bubbling up into a small pool. The room had an under-the-earth kind of smell that mixed with the essence of burning candles and smoking incense, which I could see clustered in different spots all over the room. There were no authority figures around. As I looked across the dimly lit space, I saw only a few old ladies putting spring water on their faces as they cried and whispered unintelligibly. I was inside an old Orthodox church, and while I did not understand it at all, somehow I felt safe.

Walking over to a cubbyhole in the corner to be alone with my thoughts, I sat down to take a rest from the cold. Right in front of me hung a picture of a man with a halo. Just like so many portraits, his eyes seemed to follow me. I looked up and whispered, "I know you can't hear me, but I really need someone to talk to right now."

I began to pour out my heart to the religious icon on the wall. Although I felt ridiculous speaking to a painting, it was a much-needed release for me. For the first time I was able to verbalize my plans and make sense of everything while offloading some of the pressure that was mounting in my mind. I knew that the wall did not have ears, but I felt listened to, and peace came to me somehow.

A few days later I returned and had another talk with my friend on the wall. All that I knew was that this guy was helping me to stay sane. Talking with him gave me the courage that I needed to combat the nagging fear that I was not going to make it. I was definitely encountering some sort of strange connection with something or someone, only later to find out that it was Jesus Himself. All along He had been right there, listening. He had been guiding me and giving me the strength I needed to make my escape. I needed to be free. I needed to live.

. . . . . .

We all need life—real life with real joy that can come only from Jesus. While I grew up in a system absent of God, today I experience God's vibrant presence daily, which has given me an ecstatic joy I love to express wherever I go. Perhaps you have picked up this book because you are looking for this kind of joy. True exuberant joy begins when you encounter the living Jesus. Let me share with you some of my backstory and my initial encounter with Him.

Born into a Joyless, Godless Land

In 1944, just four years before I was born, a violent revolution began tearing up many of the eastern European countries, and Bulgaria was one of them. My grandfathers on both sides of the family had been successful. One was a banker and the other owned a large refinery. The Communists stepped in and confiscated their businesses and their properties. This happened to all business owners, and those who resisted were murdered, many by public execution. While my grandfathers were allowed to live, they were jailed and beaten. No one dared to tell me exactly what had happened. I knew nothing about my family history or identity. Everything was hush-hush. Only the official Marxist propaganda could be spoken aloud.

We were living and breathing, but it felt as though we were buried alive inside a giant societal tomb. We were closed off from the West, and the government, media and KGB enforced our entombment. Suspicion was looming everywhere. We knew that eyes and ears were always watching and always listening, just waiting for us to say or do the wrong thing. One of my school friends was arrested and interrogated until they found out how he got the fancy shoes he was wearing. The shoes were foreign, and that had made him a suspect. The logic was that if someone gave you a pair of foreign shoes, then you must be colluding with the West. After all, capitalism was corrupt, evil influences needed to be blocked, and those shoes posed a real threat.

Religion was another threat. They called it "the opiate of the masses," and we were all brainwashed to be good atheists. Bibles were confiscated before I was born, and the printing plates for the Bible were destroyed so that no one could ever make another copy. I never heard the Scriptures growing up. I never heard the Lord's name spoken aloud.

Just like everyone else's, my family was poor. We lived in a little room inside my grandparents' apartment on my father's side of the family. Each night we cooked a pot of potatoes, sat together and peeled them while they were hot, and then sprinkled them with spices. We ate together, and yet I do not remember my mother being with us. My parents rarely spoke to one another. Somehow, she stayed away from my father and his family. By the time I reached five years of age, my mother took me to live in a small room in someone else's apartment. My parents got a divorce, and I never saw my father much after that. My mother continued to move me around the city. We moved fifteen times during my childhood; I switched schools twelve times in eleven years. This made it nearly impossible to make friends or grow roots. No matter where we lived, the neighborhood boys playing ball outside my window were far out of reach because my mother insisted that I take violin lessons and spend my afternoon practicing scales and arpeggios instead. Without my father, and without any connection to the kids at school or in the neighborhoods, I was left with a tremendous void inside.

At school, nothing made sense. I was left-handed, and because this was illegal and forbidden by the Communists, the teachers forced me to learn how to write with my right hand. I could never understand why. When I asked my mother, all that she could say was, "Well, that's what they want you to do, so go ahead and learn to use your right hand, Georgi." My grades dropped. I was practically failing out of school. Everything seemed pointless. I was barely existing and became growingly detached from life itself.

Discovering Freedom in Music

When rock-and-roll music hit Western Europe in the early 1960s, I discovered the Beatles. Most summers, my mother sent me to live with her parents. It was always a big break for me. I enjoyed my time with them, plus away from my mother's watchful eye, I got to play outside with my cousins and other boys from the neighborhood instead of practicing my violin every day.

No one knew that my grandfather owned an illegal shortwave radio, which he kept hidden in the basement. I discovered his secret and would often sneak downstairs late at night while everyone was sound asleep. Turning the radio on quietly and cautiously, I could hear illegal broadcasts piped in from the West. As I fiddled with the dials, all of a sudden, I heard the music of John, Paul, George and Ringo for the very first time in my life. They took my breath away. I was mesmerized by their irresistible melodies and rhythms, instantly bringing some excitement and joy into my miserable life.

Even though the Communists jammed the frequencies with ear-splitting noises and interruptions, nothing could discourage me from listening. These radical new sounds were captivating. Eventually I shared this forbidden pleasure with three musician friends, and it ignited the fire of our youthful passions. In 1964 we formed the first official rock band in Bulgaria and called ourselves *Srebyrnite Grivni* (the Silver Bracelets). I played the drums and sang.

In 1965 we made our debut on national television. Instantly we became an overnight sensation for we were the first of our kind. Youth everywhere were drawn to this new electric sound. I am sure the managers of the television station thought nothing of broadcasting our seemingly harmless teenage band.

Because there was only one television channel in all of Bulgaria, the entire nation saw us on prime time. Now the cat was out of the bag; youth everywhere were immediately drawn in by this new sound. Rock music became a vehicle my generation could use to build our own identities. It also offered us an opportunity to rebel and vent all of our frustrations. We had never

24

wanted to claim Lenin as our father; with this new Lennon, we identified with someone cool, wild and free.

We pushed against the limits every chance we could get. The Communists had given us a temporary license to play soft melodic folk music *only*. Our concerts were always under their supervision. They would turn our levels down whenever they thought we were too loud, and they restricted our audience from clapping *during* our songs; it was only after the song had ended that they would be allowed to "applaud." At heart we were a progressively raw, wild and rebellious, rock-and-roll band—and that forced us underground so that we could be true to our music. We were plugged in, pulsating and loud. Young people, hearing about us by word of mouth, came to our illegal concerts in droves. They shouted, danced, clapped and raised their hands throughout our entire performances.

Word must have gotten out, because shockwaves hit the Bulgarian Communist party. We were now a serious threat. It was as if invisible sparks were inciting our crowds. Fearing that our concerts were starting to smolder with the fire of revolution, the government banned us from playing in public and outlawed our music.

Plotting My Escape

This pushed me beyond my limits. There was absolutely no way that I could go back to the colorless life the Communists had plotted out for me. Rock music had allowed me to breathe fresh air for the first time; I simply could not be sealed back inside that stifling tomb again. Even though I had to go through the motions of daily life, I never lost my determination to find a way out of their clutches. From the moment they shut down our music, escape was always on my mind. I began plotting my way out.

It took me a couple of years to come up with a formidable plan. In the meantime I served in the army and went to college. I never felt like a rebel or a revolutionary; I simply felt like a slave. In due time, I was going to find out that it was actually God Himself who fueled this yearning for freedom deep inside of me. It was also God who equipped me with everything I needed to make my escape.

When I received my two-year degree from music college, my mom decided to send me to East Germany as a reward for graduating with honors. She also needed me to buy some art supplies, which could only be found in Germany. So to East Berlin I went.

One evening I wandered into a nightclub where I bumped into an old rock-and-roll friend of mine, a guitarist from Bulgaria named Mitar. We were both surprised to see each other. He told me that he was playing with a German band at one of the clubs.

"By the way," he said, "we could really use a drummer. Want to join the band?"

My first thought was, *I'm looking for freedom, not more of the same restrictions*, but I kept my thoughts to myself and agreed to meet him for lunch the next day.

The city was divided by the Berlin Wall, which separated the Communist East from the democratic West. We were at the height of the Cold War. The United States, the United Kingdom and France were all protecting their interests on the Western side. On the Eastern side, the Soviet Union controlled the border guards, and they were ruthless. It was like standing in the middle of a showdown, a clash between two worlds at war. In addition to the Wall, anyone who fancied a venture to West Berlin faced a high-voltage electric fence, trained attack dogs and machine guns at every block ready to shoot you. All in all, this was the most suicidal spot to attempt an escape.

I met Mitar for lunch that next day at a rotating restaurant atop the Fernsehturm, a television tower and the tallest structure in Germany. From that height you could see West Berlin. On my side of the wall, everything was gray and pale like death. Looking over to the other side, into freedom, I could see that people were filled with life. It seemed as though they were pulsating with energy and vibrant colors. I had never seen freedom before, and I wanted it.

I said to my friend, "Why play in East Germany when we could play with the free people over there, where everything would be so much better?" At that moment we secretly agreed to escape together.

I went back home to Sofia saying that I would be applying to the musical conservatory in Berlin. In actuality, I had just gotten a six-month contract to play in a German band with Mitar, and this would give us the time that we needed to work out the details of our escape. I turned in my band contract at the visa department in Sofia and waited for my papers to be processed.

It was during this time that I wandered into the warmth of that old Orthodox church in the cave. I was in great turmoil knowing that I would soon leave everything I had known behind, for good, and that I would be putting my life on the line to find freedom. Whispering to that picture of the man with a halo gave me the strength and courage I needed during my wait.

Finally, in 1972, my visa came in. I packed my little bag and fought back tears as I kissed the Bulgarian girl that I had fallen in love with goodbye. We had been planning to marry, but I said goodbye to her, my mom and my relatives and headed for Berlin.

It did not take Mitar and me long to come up with our plan. Looking back at the series of twists and turns that would ultimately take us to freedom, it becomes obvious that the Lord was charting our course.

We had decided to make our way out through the Yugoslavian border. Because of a rift between dictators Tito and Stalin, Yugoslavia had managed to maintain autonomy from the Soviet Union. Her borders were soft when compared to others. The guards would certainly try to catch you, but Tito forbade them to shoot anyone. So if they could not catch you, you were free.

The hard part was getting into Yugoslavia from any of the countries tightly sealed behind the Iron Curtain. If we could make it through, we knew that we would be able to cross over to freedom in Vienna very easily.

And that is what happened. Through a series of crazy-miraculous events, my friend and I followed a secret black market route through Yugoslavia into Austria, and escaped the Iron Curtain.

Austria was an anomaly during the Cold War. While connected to the West culturally and economically, it was politically restrained from joining NATO. That meant we could not stay. We were allowed only six months to find asylum before we had to leave the country. The problem was, as we went from embassy to embassy Mitar and I were turned down. Holland, England, West Germany and Canada rejected us. Perhaps their quotas were already full, but, regardless, we were growing disheartened.

Welcome to America, Boys

In our minds there were just two more embassies to try: Australia and the United States of America. Australia seemed much too far away, while America was known to be much more generous in accepting immigrants. The Russians, however, had indoctrinated us to believe that the Americans were our worst enemies, and that America was the most evil place on earth. Feeling as though we had no choice, we headed reluctantly to the American embassy. We were frightened to death.

As we told our story to the guards at the gate, they connected us with someone inside the embassy. Before we knew it, we were standing in front of the consulate. Listening to our escape story, he stood up with open arms and said, "Welcome to America, boys. We like your kind. You risked your lives for freedom, and that is what America is built on: immigrants just like you."

I gasped and tears filled my eyes. In that moment my fears were melted by this warm and sincere welcome. Suddenly our enemies were not our enemies at all. I was undone.

In due time I was aboard an American plane with my friend Mitar. We were flying over the Atlantic Ocean with one-way tickets for New York paid for by the Tolstoy Foundation. I was very eager to go to Hollywood, where I thought the action was, for my heart was set on pursuing rock and roll. Because I did not speak English, the foundation was going to help me find a job.

It took me a full year to make my way across the United States; Mitar and I parted ways in pursuit of our respective dreams. First, I worked in Sarasota, Florida, where I dug ditches in the hot sun every day and then washed dishes at night for a seafood place. I went up to Detroit to work on an automobile assembly line, where I could work overtime and make lots of money quickly. Once I had saved enough to make my way to California, I started my journey in an old beat-up mail truck. Little did I know as I drove out West that the God I did not believe in was waiting for me there.

Encountering Jesus People in Hollywood

I was finally living in a free country, but somehow I still did not feel very free on the inside. I could not understand the dull ache gnawing at me. After all, I had made it to California and was now free to pursue my dreams. But the truth was I was still looking for something beautiful and fulfilling. Nothing was turning out the way I thought it would be. I walked Hollywood's Walk of Fame and saw drug dealers and prostitutes everywhere. I even witnessed winos vomiting on the stars on the sidewalk.

I thought, *Wow, I risked my life to get here. This is not worth living and dying for.*

God waited for my dreams to crash, and then He introduced me to some young hippies on the streets of Ojai, California— real Jesus freaks. It was the tail end of the Jesus movement in the early 1970s, and revival was breaking out among many young people. This group in particular went out on the streets every day, sharing the joy and peace they had found in Jesus. They also ran a house for people recovering from drug and alcohol abuse.

Every time I saw them, they said things like "Jesus loves you—He really does" and "He died for you!"

I remember thinking, *What kind of drugs are they on?* They would smile and look at me with dreamy stares. Later on I would understand that God's joy, peace and love were pouring out of their eyes and radiating irresistibly in the frequencies of their voices.

I think they realized that this Bulgarian guy's love language was food. I may have been a total atheist, but I was also broke and always famished. They invited me to come and eat with them the next day. I certainly did not believe in anything they were talking about, but I was happy to join them to eat a good meal.

Once they learned that I was a musician, they pulled out their instruments and began playing their music for me. I was astounded, but not in a good way. Their guitars, their piano and their flute were all painfully out of tune.

As they played, I was thinking, *What is wrong with them? Don't they know how bad they sound?* It drove me nuts. I was cringing inside, hoping that they would stop and take a tuning break. To make matters worse, all of their songs used only three chords (C, D and G) and they rotated between these three chords all night long.

My thoughts kept churning: *They should be crying right now after playing such pathetic music. Yet for some reason they are excited, and behaving as though they are playing for a sold-out stadium.*

They did not seem to notice my reaction because they were completely lost in their music. I, on the other hand, was wondering what was wrong with this picture. I had a musical background, but I sat there feeling completely miserable. They were clearly not accomplished musicians, but they were filled with joy and happiness.

When they finally finished, they put down their instruments and asked, "So what did you think, Georgian?"

I desperately wanted to say, *Give me whatever drug you are on that makes you feel so good for no reason; I want it right now!* Instead, I mumbled something just to be polite. After all, dinner was about to be served. They were persistent in reminding me at every opportunity, "Jesus loves you," and they continued inviting me to dinner.

God Encounter on the Mountain

Every day I would think, *Endure all of that just for a free meal? No way!*

But by six o'clock the hunger pains would hit, and I would find myself back in their house listening to really bad music just

31

so I could fill my belly with their good food. After two months, I finally said to myself, *I can't do this anymore. I don't believe a word of what they are saying about this Jesus. I'm just eating their food. It's time to go down to Hollywood to pursue my career in rock music. But out of respect for all of their efforts, I'll give it a chance—just in case there is some truth to what they are saying.*

Wanting to be alone, I followed some trails that took me up one of the nearest mountains. Unsure of what to do or say exactly, my mind was going crazy: *What are you doing? How can you talk to someone that you don't believe is there? This is so stupid; I don't know what to say.*

I had already had full conversations with that painting of a man on the wall back in Sofia, so I am not sure why I was having so much trouble.

Then unexpectedly, a question floated up in my mind: *God, do You exist?*

I thought, *Great, a perfect question. It will prove that He really doesn't exist. Go ahead. Say it and get it over with.* So, alone on that mountaintop, I said it out loud, certain that no one could hear me: "God, do You exist?"

Boom! As soon as I uttered those words, something happened. It felt as if I got covered by a canopy or blanket of some sort. I was stunned. I could feel someone or something all around me. Even the acoustics of the mountain air changed. The presence that surrounded me became thicker and more palpable. I began to shake.

"What is happening?" I cried out. Suddenly, the revelation that God actually exists ran through me like a lightning bolt. All of my life, I had listened to the Communist's lies. They had lied about everything; it should have dawned on me that they would lie about God, too. It was unmistakably true: God *does* exist!

I shook so hard that I fell down into the dirt. I shook and cried all day on that mountaintop, merely from the discovery that there really is a God.

"Who are You?" I cried out. "What are You? I can't see You, but I can tell that You are there!"

The more I talked, the thicker the presence became. I was crying loudly, desperately wanting to know more about this invisible God whose presence I could somehow feel. I had an overwhelming desire to know everything immediately.

Hours passed. Finally, I realized that it was starting to grow dark and cold. While there was still enough light to find my way down the mountain, I knew that I had to go to the house where the Jesus People were.

My eyes and face were swollen from crying all day. They opened the front door, took one look at me and smiled knowingly. "Ahhh, Georgian, come on in!" This time, I did not go to the kitchen. I wanted to join them in the living room where they played their music because I now understood the joy of playing for this invisible God.

The Hands of Jesus and the Holy Spirit

They began playing their guitars energetically and singing loudly. This time I did not care what they played or how it sounded because I could now sense they were connecting with the God I had just experienced. After two months of their witnessing, this Bulgarian was finally getting it, and my new friends were ecstatic.

As they were shouting praises, I saw a vision: The hands of Jesus came toward me. I could not see His face, but I could see His hands. I fell right into them and landed facedown on the carpet as Jesus wrapped His loving arms around me. His peace and love melted me and filled me. From that moment on, I had an insatiable hunger and thirst for His presence. Once I had tasted these things, the thought of never having them again was unbearable. He became my oxygen.

The following day my friends said, "We are so excited for you, Georgian. Now you should ask the Lord to fill you with the Holy Spirit."

"The Holy Spirit?" I asked. I had no idea what they were talking about.

"Oh, yeah, ask God to baptize you in His Spirit and power. Just you wait and see. It's going to be great!"

I did everything that I could think of to ask for the Holy Spirit, but nothing happened. I returned to my friends to ask them what was wrong.

"Nothing is wrong," they said. "Just keep asking and soon you will feel Him."

I walked away and asked again for the Holy Spirit. I waited but still nothing happened. I came back and questioned my friends again, "Is this Holy Spirit part of God or what?"

"Yes, yes," they told me, "Wait, you'll see. Just ask Him to fill you."

I continued asking over and over again for nearly a week, but nothing happened.

Finally, I said to my friends, "Be honest and tell me what's wrong. Something has to be wrong with me because I'm asking but I'm not getting anything."

They said, "Chill out, Georgian, there's nothing wrong with you, man. You've been a Communist all your life. It's been less than a week, you have to just keep asking and—"

"*Don't tell me to chill out!*" I shouted. "I lost my family and career because of those Communists. I want everything I've missed out on, and I want it all right now! Is it for me and is it good?"

"Yes," they replied.

"Well, then, I want it now!" I said emphatically. "Don't talk to me anymore about this Holy Ghost unless I get it. I need to have it right *now*, or I don't want to hear another word about it."

Having been constrained by the Communists for most of my life, I had a very intense attitude about getting those things I had missed.

The Throne Room

"All right, Georgian," they said. "We will pray for you."

Before they started to pray, I began hearing a sound. It grew louder and surrounded me. I heard thousands of cheering voices, louder than a stadium full of yelling fans. Then I saw a curtain open, and when I looked through it, I could actually see heaven. I was at the edge of the throne room and started to enter.

There were swarms of angels, swirling and squealing in uncontained ecstasy. They had their backs to me, and even though I could not see their faces I could hear the sounds of ecstatic pleasure coming from them. God was on His throne and completely surrounded by adoring angels.

Wow! I marveled. *They're having a really good time.*

Next, I saw lightning and fire come out of God. It hit the angels, who could barely handle all of the pleasure. Their wriggling and fluttering swelled with every jolt they received from Him. I had never read the Bible, of course, and no one ever told me about Psalm 16:11, which says, "In Your presence is fullness of joy; in Your right hand there are pleasures forever."

Awestruck, I continued watching, and without warning one of the lightning flashes from God headed toward me. As it neared my chest and before it struck me, I saw it as a grapefruit-sized fireball. Then it went inside my body.

It is difficult to find words to describe what I experienced. It was as if fire, love, joy and pleasure entered me all at once. It was amazingly good, but, in a way, it was too good. I actually wished God would tone it down a notch or two. I could not handle that much. Yet before I knew it, a second fireball was coming straight at me.

Now it was getting *very* intense. As this deluge of pleasure passed through me, I began acting just like the angels—wriggling, jumping and spinning around.

Bob was the person standing and praying behind me. I turned and hugged him hard and said, "Bob, I love you! I love you! I really love you!" I was squeezing him and raving, "I have this love, Bob! Can't you tell?"

He said, "Ah, yeah, man, I know you love me."

"Oh, no, Bob," I said. "Can't you feel it . . . the fire and the love? I have this amazing new love. It's the love of God. There's this fire everywhere. Can't you see it, can't you feel it, Bob?"

It was getting hotter and stronger, so I ran outside to cool off, but it only increased. Then I panicked because of the intensity of my experience, and asked the Lord to stop. He stopped immediately. Once released from that incredible feeling, I was instantly sorry and asked myself, *Why did I panic like that? It was so good!* My friends had never mentioned the fire, so I was not sure if I was getting the right thing. Their instructions were about tongues, not fire. I could not speak in tongues at that point. All I could do was scream. I had really thought I would die if God had turned it up one more degree.

I learned an invaluable lesson from this: Never ask the Lord to stop. Now I know to say, "More, Lord. Just strengthen my inner man to handle Your consuming presence."

After that experience with the Lord, my life would never be the same. He baptized me with His fiery love, and my heart was forever branded with an insatiable hunger for Him. Someone bought me a Bulgarian Bible and I began to devour His Word. I spent hours and hours every day reading, meditating on every page and talking with God. Each Old Testament story was like watching a movie. It was as if the Lord took me back in time to observe every scene unfold. I encountered Jesus in His people, through His presence and in His Word.

Encountering Jesus

Starting life in a brand-new country did not complete my escape. I often tell people that *even though you could take me out of Communism, it was an entirely different matter to take Communism out of me!*

It was not until I gave my life to Jesus that I found the freedom, peace and joy that I had been yearning for. Bottom line, the greatest thing on earth is to encounter Jesus—everything else pales in comparison. Maybe you haven't? Each one of us has a story; we have all experienced some sort of Iron Curtain situation that we need to be rescued from. What He came to do for me, He will do for you, too. Why not ask Him now if you have not already? He is waiting with open arms and ready to help you, too.

In the pages ahead, I will share how eager I was to be His grateful *servant*, willing to do anything for Him. But He was about to show me what it meant to be His *friend*.

2
Friendship with God

Now I knew that God existed. He was really real. Having just experienced His love, fire and ecstatic joy, an insatiable hunger for more of Him consumed me. He was good, He loved me, and I needed more. I needed to know everything about Him. I was desperate to make up for all of the time I had lost because of those lying Communists.

I found a cheap apartment and a part-time job making pizza and popcorn at a local theater. This provided enough free food and just enough money to pay my meager bills.

Now I could give maximum time to Jesus. It was in that little studio apartment that I devoted myself to studying God's Word eight, nine, ten hours a day for an entire year, reading through the Bible multiple times from cover to cover.

With so many questions, I did not want to rush my way through. Starting with the first chapter of Genesis, I read slowly, all the while talking to Jesus. One of my earliest questions was, "How do I pray?" Everything was new to me.

I understood protocol from my service in the Bulgarian army. If a high-ranking officer entered the room, you did not just blurt words out or do whatever you wanted. You were under his authority; it was up to him to set the tone and direct the course of action. This is why a soldier stands at attention and waits for orders.

I wanted to know how to properly approach the God of the universe, the Ruler of all things. What was His code of conduct? Surely there had to be etiquette. That was when I heard Him tell me to open up my Bible to the pages in the middle.

There He instructed me, *Start reading the chapters out loud, Georgian. That's how you can pray to Me.*

David Prayed like a Friend of God

In the center of my Bible I found the book of Psalms and started to read. I was surprised to discover how bold these conversations were. I had already read about David in First and Second Samuel, and I discovered that he was one of the main authors of these poetic chapters. He was an amazing warrior and king, but before that he was a lonely kid seemingly rejected by his father, just like me. I connected with him on that level, but it shocked me to see him sharing such honest emotions with the Lord. I felt awkward reading his grievances and anxieties out loud.

Page by page, I choked a little, but I hung in there and continued to speak the psalms back to the Lord: "I am weary with my sighing; every night I make my bed swim, I dissolve my couch with my tears. My eye has wasted away with grief; it has become old because of all my adversaries" (Psalm 6:6–7).

David continued to express his feelings, and there was an array of them. One time in his distress, he even accused the Lord of abandoning him: "How long, O LORD? Will you forget me forever? How long will you hide your face from me?" (Psalm 13:1 GWT).

Because my father was never present in my life, I detected something that surprised me as David cried out for protection. Though I felt that it was not the right way to speak to the Lord, I could hear the raw pain of abandonment in David's cry, and I realized that was what the Lord heard, too.

Rich in mercy, the Lord did not strike David with lightning or quit on him during the emotional turbulence. In the psalms that followed, I could see that the dam had burst and a breakthrough had come. David was now singing the high praises of God, exuberantly declaring Him an ever-present help in times of trouble. The Lord heard the cry of David's heart and answered him in ways that defied David's imagination. Not only did the Lord rescue David and crush all of his enemies, He also crushed David's personal insecurities and filled that void within him with His steadfast, never-ever-going-to-leave-you kind of love.

I came to realize that David was a friend of God, and that true friends can share their hearts with one another—they are not afraid to. This gave me courage to push through my own fears and insecurities. As I began to understand the depths of God's inexhaustible kindness and goodness, I, too, began to speak with Him like a friend.

This was a radical marker for me. I continued to study the Bible systematically, chapter by chapter, but I also took time to read and pray the psalms every day. I found myself being secured into a wonderful friendship with a loving God, who in His compassion would hear and answer whenever I cried out to Him.

My heart often swelled with both tears and laughter. Having noticed that so many of the psalms were meant to be sung, I began strumming my guitar and serenaded God with adoring verses over and over again.

God Befriended Abraham

My days were filled with adventure as I spent time with my Lord reading His Word and asking questions. He helped me to see everything like a movie. It was supernatural, like being transported back through time and watching everything in high definition with surround sound. As the stories unfolded, the Bible became alive to me.

I particularly loved Abraham and his wife, Sarah. He was a foreigner in a strange land just like me. He became God's friend because the Lord spoke with him and spent time with him. One day the Lord even sat down in an atmosphere of fellowship to eat a meal that Abraham and Sarah had prepared for Him. I was mesmerized reading this story. They lived in a tent in the middle of the desert. Their food had to be made from scratch, which took a lot of time. They had to kill a calf, skin it, butcher it, season it and then cook it over a fire. They also had to knead and bake the bread. My imagination ran wild.

I asked the Lord how He could possibly have taken the time to sit under the oak tree and wait while they prepared that meal for Him. After all, He was in charge of so many things. Surely He was much too busy for something like that.

I sensed Him explaining this to me: *How else can human beings understand friendship except through time? You have to click through the clock together. That's what friends do—they enjoy each other by spending time in each other's company.*

That is when it hit me: Although God has many important things to do, He was doing the same thing with me. He was present in my room, answering all of my questions—just so that He could spend time with me. We were friends, too!

Bowled over, I could not contain myself. I decided to invite the Lord to a meal, just like Abraham. I went into my kitchenette and put together what I had, frying up potatoes and bacon bits. I tried to bake some bread, but it came out of my tiny oven almost as hard as a rock.

I apologized and said, "I'm so sorry, Lord. You are going to have to watch Your teeth on that bread!"

I served Him the meal, along with a glass of lemonade—and I could feel Him sitting there with me. Bolstered by my devotional times in the Psalms, I was swimming out further and deeper into the ocean of His friendship.

When I read, for instance, that Abraham had negotiated with God about the destruction of Sodom and Gomorrah, I just could not fathom how someone would dare to go back and forth with God like that.

> Abraham asked him, "LORD, when you destroy the evil people, are you also going to destroy those who are good? Wouldn't you spare the city if there are only 50 good people in it?" . . . The LORD replied, "If I find 50 good people in Sodom, I will save the city to keep them from being killed."
>
> Genesis 18:23–24, 26 CEV

But Abraham did not stop there. Would the Lord spare the city if He could find 45 good people?

Yes, said the Lord. He would.

Then, Abraham pushed further, asking question after question: What about forty? . . . Thirty? . . . Twenty? . . . Ten? Each time the Lord responded that He would show mercy.

Throughout the dialogue I was frightened for Abraham, wondering what might happen to him. When I saw the positive and generous outcome, I began asking my own questions.

"Are You really allowing this human to argue with You and twist Your arm?"

Feeling His pleasure, I heard God explain, *No, that's not it—I'm actually allowing Abraham to share with Me in what I'm doing.*

Wow! That is friendship with God at a major level. I was astonished. I had just discovered intercession, where He lets us petition and partner with Him about an issue.

As I read about God befriending Abraham, having called him out of Ur in the land of the Chaldeans, a culture filled with idol worship, I could track with all of that, having grown up under Communist idolatry. As children, we were forced to march into the public square and then turn to face the Communist leaders as we raised our hands while shouting, "Glory to the Communist party." They were our false idols who controlled everything, and we were their property, their full possession.

When God first called Abraham and said, "I'll make a nation out of you," Abraham was not really a "believer" yet. God was calling forth a foreigner, and as his story and journey unfolded, I saw my own. I was called away from my homeland without even knowing that I was being called. He drew me through the passion that He had placed inside me to be free.

When God told Abraham to go out and look up into the night sky to count all of the stars, he was being called away from the enclosure of his tent so that he could see the tremendous destiny God had for him. That was the moment he became overwhelmed by what the Lord was telling him. He was made able to believe in something so much bigger, and he came into agreement with God.

Reading all this helped me understand how I came to believe, too. I started seeing everything that the Lord did just to get me to California. And then, everything He did to open up my heart to trust and believe Him. As He spoke to my heart in the story of His friendship with Abraham, He began to put value and destiny into me.

Christ Turns Enemies into Friends

I saw this recurring theme of friendship with God as I read the New Testament. In Romans, Galatians and Ephesians, the apostle Paul explains that salvation, our new birth, is an outright gift. We could never earn salvation by our own efforts, nor maintain our new life by our own abilities.

Not only is it all a gift, in 2 Corinthians I saw something powerful: Christ turns His enemies into friends. Anyone who is joined to Christ is a new being; the old is gone, and the new has come.

> All this is done by God, who through Christ changed us from enemies into his friends and gave us the task of making others his friends also. Our message is that God was making all human beings his friends through Christ. God did not keep an account of their sins, and he has given us the message which tells how he makes them his friends.
>
> 2 Corinthians 5:18–19 GNT

Even before I knew the Lord, He tested the metal of my belief system. He caused me to begin to see things in a new light. It was time for me to start considering my enemies as new friends for the making.

Coming to America was step number one. I wrote earlier how, after escaping through the Iron Curtain, my friend and I made the hard decision to go to the U.S. Embassy. I was shaking like a leaf on the inside because I believed that there was no worse place to be in the entire world than the United States of America.

Yet we were warmly welcomed and found ourselves on a plane headed for New York. After we landed, I still expected Americans to be cold, emotionless robots who only cared about making money. But while waiting for our ride we watched people greet each other with warm hugs and vibrant affection. I had never seen that kind of open display. Not quite sure what was happening to me, I had to wipe tears quickly from my eyes. All of my beliefs about Americans were being challenged. Those I had considered enemies might not really be my enemies after all—my Communist indoctrinations were being disarmed.

In the same way, He used American believers to befriend me in Ojai, California. They were kind and patient, and befriended me with His love. They infused me with value. They loved me enough to open my heart.

Now here I was, a shiny new believer. And having come from a spiritually dark, godless culture, it was very easy for me to see what was being said by stark contrast in the fifth chapter of 2 Corinthians.

From the Fall in the Garden of Eden on, we were enemies with God. But taking a closer look, I understood something more. God did not hate Adam, and Adam did not hate God. Instead, Adam was tricked and fell into the hands of the devil, the enemy of God. Because of that one act, we were all born under the enemy-of-God system, enslaved and doomed to mass-produce endless cycles of toxic strife, cruel injustice and abuse. This was not hard for me to grasp, having been born under the oppression of Communism.

Through Christ, we are befriended. He took all of our sin, all of our rejection and every last ounce of hate to the cross on our behalf. Jesus lovingly volunteered to do this; it was planned in advance for Him to die. He is the absolute best friend that one could ever have.

A Friend Who Sticks Closer than a Brother

As I continued reading my Bible, I learned from those who walked with God before me. They mentored me through their joys and victories, and their sorrows and defeats. Like David and Abraham, each one pointed my gaze to the One who gave up everything just to have me; they proved that I could always count on Jesus, the one friend who sticks closer than a brother (see Proverbs 18:24).

Having already seen that David was able to trust Jonathan more than he could trust his own siblings, it comforted me that this friendship with Jesus was a loyal connection that ran deeper than my own family relationships could ever have taken me. I was only four years old during my parents' bitter divorce. Each pitted me against the other instead of protecting me, and their personal war tore me apart. Not only did I lose my father, I lost my family. And because my mother constantly moved us around the city, I lived with a mix of strangers. I never felt secure.

Now here I was, alone in a foreign country, still feeling lonely.

From Friendship to Family

Next the Lord led me to the story of Joseph. Just like me, he was born into a dysfunctional family. I could relate to his woundedness. Joseph was betrayed and trafficked by his own brothers. They sold him as a slave to captors who took him away to a foreign land.

Many years later and after many hardships, Joseph was elevated to the second-highest position in all of Egypt. A severe famine gripped the region, including Canaan, where Joseph had come from. His brothers needed to take desperate measures to save their families. Upon hearing that there was grain available in Egypt, they travelled there hoping to find enough food to bring back to their camp.

My heart ached as I read how the brothers stood and bowed before Joseph. It was just as the prophetic dream had outlined, and yet not one of the brothers recognized him. Joseph was touched in his heart, but still carried very deep wounds from their betrayal. He concealed his identity, keeping it a secret from everyone so that he could look for signs from them. He needed to know if they carried any regret or remorse for what they had done to him. Joseph set up a series of maneuvers that would test their feelings for their youngest brother, Benjamin, who happened to be Joseph's only maternal sibling.

The trap was set, and the play was in motion. A silver cup had been planted inside Benjamin's sack of grain, and Benjamin was to be taken away as a slave because of his supposed thievery.

As all the brothers stood before Joseph, Judah cried out, "Take me as your slave instead!" It was the final straw to break Joseph's heart wide open and melt away his bitterness and unforgiveness. Judah's willingness to take Benjamin's place was a foreshadowing of Christ's saving act.

Joseph could not control himself in front of his servants any longer, so he cried out, "Have everyone leave me." When only the brothers were left with Joseph, he told them who he was. Joseph cried so loudly that the Egyptians heard him, and the people in the king's palace heard about it (see Genesis 45:1–2).

He finally revealed his identity to his astonished brothers, and all of the years of pain and resentment came out of Joseph in that moment. This is why he wept so loudly. Even though he had been severely betrayed, deep down inside his heart had always yearned for reconnection. This breakthrough caused the entire family to come from Canaan and reunite with Joseph in Egypt. The Lord invaded their broken relationships and restored them as a family. They ended up all living together with favor, provision and blessing.

Reading Joseph's story I found myself weeping, and it was loud, too. It seemed endless. And just like David, my couch became wet from my tears. The Lord was breaking through my own bitterness and sense of abandonment.

I knew what it was like to be used as a pawn in a larger game, to feel so alone, to shut down emotionally. But the Lord used Joseph's wounding to draw me in and pop me open. He broke me away from my own woundedness. Everything that had been boiling beneath the surface began pouring out of me.

To my surprise, I began crying out to the Lord for friends and family. Jesus had become my friend, but I needed to feel connected to others. I no longer wanted to be alone. Up until that point, I had been a rebel. I felt like a scared wild animal. Because I had been so mistreated, I was never able to connect with anyone—not even the Jesus People in Ojai who witnessed to me and loved me. I had never really engaged with them. I engaged by believing, but that was all.

Now, the Lord lanced my deep wound, and all the infection that had kept me isolated came pouring out.

It was time to become a part of a family.

Your Friendship with Jesus

Friendship is huge. I understood friendship—the power, the beauty and the love of it. Even though I grew up isolated and lonely, I managed to have a few solid friendships while growing up in Bulgaria. We enjoyed hanging out together, and they were like lifelines to me. To this day we are still friends, staying in touch with each other across the miles.

When God introduced Himself to me, He pursued me through friendship knowing that I could relate in that way. Gleaning from the lives of two of God's best friends, David and Abraham, I was brought into that place of deep intimate trust with the Lord. He became my best friend, and I "got" it.

A secure personal friendship with Jesus is vital to entering sonship. It makes you healthy and allows you to enter into healthy relationships with your brothers and sisters in the Lord. The Lord had won me over and was about to show me that I was ready to become a part of a much larger family with a heavenly Father. If you are having a difficult time trusting the Lord, my encouragement to you is to give Him a chance to be your best friend, and to love you closer than a brother. He is the most faithful and loyal friend that you will ever find.

3
Discovering God as Father

I began attending Sunday services at a local church in Ventura. They had invited Winkie Pratney, a well-respected youth evangelist, to speak one morning. As he taught from the platform, I found myself hanging on his every word. He seemed to know a lot about God, and there was also a spark of joy and childlike fun in his spirit. I thought to myself that, even if it meant carrying his bags so that I could follow him everywhere, I would love to hear more from this man.

As soon as the service was over, I approached Winkie. He was very kind and took some time to answer my questions and to pray with me. After a hearty amen, he looked me in the eye and invited me to attend the school in Santa Rosa, California, where he taught. I felt that the Lord's peace was on this idea, so without hesitation, I packed up and moved to Santa Rosa to join the Agape Force Discipleship Training School.

During one of my first classes, a visiting guest teacher explained that today's lesson was going to be about prayer. My ears perked up. Prayer and reading the Bible had become my top two favorite things. My excitement fizzled out, however, when he began to describe prayer as hard work. He then went on to compare it to digging ditches. Our class ended with these instructions: "Get your shovels out and start digging."

While I could not speak English nearly as well as everyone else in the room, I certainly understood ditch digging. One of my military exercises in the Bulgarian army was to dig a ditch deep and wide enough to bury a Russian tank. That was blistering hard work, and it did not line up with my prayer experience at all. It dawned on me that this instructor did not enjoy praying.

Our days were packed with classes, ministry activities and chores that kept us on a tight schedule. We were to devote an hour in the mornings to prayer, but I personally longed for more time with the Lord than that. Because our dinners were not mandatory, I decided to skip my evening meals so that I could take long walks at night to pray and spend luxurious hours with Jesus.

I was getting to know and love so many of the powerful leaders and pastors at the school. They were an amazing group of people who loved God deeply. As I grew closer to this wonderful community of believers, they embraced me and drew me into fellowship with them. For the first time in my life, I found myself belonging to a family. This had been the cry of my heart ever since I read about Joseph's reunion with his family in Egypt. God was filling my deep void, and I could not have been happier.

At the same time, I noticed a young lady who was also taking prayer walks at night. Her name was Winnie Cook, and she had just become a full-time member of the ministry after her graduation from the school. Winnie and her team were reaching out to children in the surrounding poor neighborhoods. They would feed the children pizza and donuts, and then used art and entertainment to introduce Jesus to them. At that time, there were not many kid-friendly Christian songs or materials. They often used popular Disney themes adapted to include a Gospel message.

Ministry Explosion

That is when I was invited onto a team to write and compose Christian songs for children. While none of us had ever done anything like that before, the Lord was leading us to meet this simple need. I was able to write melodies, and since English was not my strong suit, Winnie came alongside to help me write the lyrics. We ended up collaborating on three songs together: "Kindness," "Gentleness" and "Smile."

It became apparent that music and the dramatic arts were a viable way to reach the masses with the Gospel. Agape Force had always been focused on street evangelism, but things were changing. This was the mid-1970s, and contemporary Christian music was just starting to come on the scene. Up until this point, there were only pianos, organs and hymnals in churches. But the Jesus People movement introduced guitars and drums into the mix for worship, and it was revolutionary.

To accommodate this growing vision, the ministry moved its base from Northern California to Texas, where there was room to grow all of these God dreams. Because of my background in classical and rock-and-roll music, I was invited to participate in many of their projects.

While I had met Winnie once or twice before, she continued to help me write lyrics during several songwriting projects. She made me feel special, and I started to grow more and more fond of this beautiful young lady.

The ministry began producing albums for children, and the three songs that Winnie and I had written together ended up on the first one—*Music Machine*. It was an adventurous kind of musical experience for children that taught them about the fruit of the Spirit.

We were thrilled to be a part of this pioneering project—nothing like this had ever been done before. To our amazement, *Music Machine* took off like a rocket and became the first album in the Christian market to go platinum, meaning it sold more than one million copies.

We continued working with the team and produced a series of children's albums, including *Bullfrogs and Butterflies*. The series won several Dove Awards and Grammy nominations and went Triple Platinum (more than three million copies sold). And the outreach did not stop there. The albums were followed by books, an animated video game and even *Music Machine* movies.

We loved writing and producing music for children, but we had a growing desire to reach adults as well with our music. One of the results was the band Silverwind. I became one of the singers, along with Betsy Hernandez and Angela Watley. Angela went on to become a missionary and was replaced by Patty Forney (Gramling). We had a Euro Pop sound and were often compared to the band ABBA.

This was the time when new trails were being blazed in Christian music. We were the generation that saw Woodstock; music was exploding with possibilities. We seemed to be moving constantly—releasing albums and playing large concert halls, arenas and music festivals.

At the end of every concert I would speak to the audiences about my escape from Communism and how I found Christ in Southern California through the Jesus People. That was our outreach format: worshipful music, testimonies from the band and then my escape story with an altar call.

I was finally able to use my musical gifts again, something I had not been able to do since my escape through the Iron Curtain. It was so fulfilling. Our music was being used to influence a generation and change lives for eternity, quite the contrast from my old days in Bulgaria. There is no way to describe the profound fulfillment of being able to put your arms around young men who were weeping at the altar and pray with them. We all found so much purpose and meaning in serving the Lord this way.

The proverbial cherry on top was that I had also fallen in love with Winnie. Even though I really loved her, I was dragging my feet and it took me a while to propose. I finally asked her to marry me once the Lord showed me that I was harboring fear because of my parents' divorce. He assured me and helped me break through by promising me that I would never know the sting of divorce again.

The first six months of our married life were spent on a tour bus.

Our daughter, Yana, was born a few years later. We were now living in Tacoma, Washington, because the Agape Force had moved its base once again.

When Winnie was seven months pregnant, we returned to Texas for a conference. While sleeping at our hotel, she woke up in an enormous pool of blood. Winnie was rushed off by ambulance. Little did we know that we were heading to the very hospital where two world-renowned experts on placenta issues were on staff.

It turns out that Yana's umbilical cord never connected to the placenta; it attached to the uterine wall instead. Miraculously, thousands of tiny hair-like vessels grew and stretched between the placenta and the umbilical cord. This kept the baby fed with the nutrients and oxygen that her little body needed to grow and develop. These vessels were so fine that they never showed up on an ultrasound, and so no one was aware. Given the unique situation, both baby and mom started to bleed out when the doctors started to deliver Yana by Caesarean birth.

It took some doing, but they were able to stabilize Yana, who entered the world at just three and a half pounds. Winnie, on the other hand, was in extreme danger. She had already lost two and a half times the amount of blood that her body needed; they pumped blood into her as fast as they could.

I learned later that blood needs to be warmed before a transfusion because it is kept in the refrigerator. Because Winnie had already received multiple rapid transfusions, blood was being pumped into her cold because there was no time to warm it. Her body started to react. Winnie's organs were shutting down.

I was in the hospital with a pastor friend. We were crying and praying when suddenly, we each heard the Lord at the same time: *Stop whining and take authority over the spirit of death. Now!* We were stunned, and we immediately did what the Lord had said to do.

The doctors did amazing work and took extraordinary measures as they fought to save her life. We did our part, too, and by God's grace and intervention, my wife's life was saved. The doctors kept both Winnie and Yana in the hospital for another month before clearing them to go home.

Silverwind was back on the road at last, and now baby Yana was an additional member on the tour bus. We were growing in popularity, ministering to sell-out crowds, and thousands were getting saved. Yet I was longing for something more. I realized that the mission field was starting to burn in my heart.

I was now the band's leader, and I shared my passion for missions. Amazingly, everyone was in full agreement. It took a year to plan, but finally we were headed for a missionary tour. I had to raise revenue and work out many details, but soon we were on our way to Kenya, Uganda, South Africa, Poland, Germany, France and Holland.

"My Jesus" or the "Bible Jesus"?

One of the most life-changing stops that we made on this missionary tour was to the war-torn nation of Uganda. The entire country had been devastated by dictator Idi Amin, who had committed mass genocide on his own people.

We played on the large steps of a famous school in Jinja, and thousands came to our concert. We should have been finishing our last song, but the Lord told us not to stop: *Just keep singing until I tell you*, He said.

His presence was incredibly strong; I saw His hands tenderly embracing all of the people.

Ten years later a missionary who had been at that event explained the magnitude of what had happened. We had no idea that our stage was on one of the exact spots where hundreds of people were slaughtered; that stage and its stairs had been covered in fountains of blood. This missionary went on to say that he believes the Lord sanctified that place and was removing the horror through our corporate worship.

In Kampala, the capital, we rented the largest soccer stadium in the city for three nights. We could hear machine guns from the guerrilla warfare off in the distance, but we experienced incredible peace. Night after night the Lord blanketed His people with His presence as we sang.

The new president's son came to speak to us personally. "Thank you for bringing the message of peace to us when we so desperately needed it," he said. "No one else has come to visit us since the genocide began. Thank you for not being afraid."

Each night at the end, I gave a fifteen-minute sermon and then an altar call. Mobs of people came forward for salvation, but they also came forward with desperate needs. I was encountering raw humanity in crisis, and I simply was not prepared. One woman brought her baby right to me. The young child was disfigured and suffering in pain.

The mother cried out, "Please heal my baby!"

I prayed for her baby, of course, but on the inside I recoiled, knowing that I did not have faith for this. I was not equipped. Even though the Lord had healed my wife and daughter, I did not know or understand very much about healing.

Still, in spite of all of our personal inadequacies, people were getting healed and touched by the Lord in Kampala. God's presence was strong, and word was spreading. People were walking in from other villages and cities hungry for God. All of us on the team were heartbroken to find out that after we left, the stadium continued to fill up for another three nights with people waiting for us to come.

My world was being rocked by all of this. The Lord was challenging me to the depths of my being. It was dawning on me that I needed a major upgrade. "My Jesus" was winning souls, but not healing people. I needed the "Bible Jesus," who also did miracles and healed people.

I prayed, "Lord, expand my faith. I know You as Savior, but I need to know You as Healer and Miracle Worker, too."

As we returned home, I felt victorious because we had accomplished something major. We had brought a contemporary Christian band to several developing nations, without even the basic infrastructure to transport or handle our sound equipment and gear, and we had delivered a first-class worship experience. That was phenomenal.

Yet, a divine tension was building, and in a short amount of time, Winnie and I would soon find ourselves standing before a new set of crossroads in our lives.

Reckon Yourself

We went back on tour in the U.S., and while we were performing a concert in Florida, one of the local pastors and organizers noticed that I was not quite myself. Winnie and I had been unable to shake this feeling of being called to something new; we were feeling unsettled. He asked me if something was troubling me. After I had confided in him briefly, he prayed and then assured me that when our plane landed back in Seattle, the Lord would give both Winnie and me an answer.

Later, as our plane touched down, I asked Winnie if she had heard anything from the Lord.

"Yes," she said. "He highlighted Abraham and Sarah, who left their country and kin behind for the land that the Lord was about to show them."

"Wow," I replied, "that's interesting!" The Lord had spoken to me the verse about needing a new wineskin in order to store new wine:

"And who would use old wineskins to store new wine? For the old skins would burst with the pressure, and the wine would be spilled and skins ruined. Only new wineskins are used to store new wine. That way both are preserved."

Matthew 9:17 TLB

It was clear that change was coming. We truly believed that the Lord was calling us to leave the band and the ministry behind. This was not an easy step to take, but Winnie encouraged me continually with the reminder that we needed to trust the Lord. Just like Abraham and Sarah, the Lord was taking us to a new place. We did not need to have it all figured out; we just needed to trust the Lord, and He would do the leading and guiding.

I performed with Silverwind for the very last time in Pasadena, and the very next morning the Lord visited me during my devotions. I had experienced His personal presence many times before, but this encounter was uniquely different. I was keenly aware that Jesus had just entered my room as *Rabboni*, the Teacher.

I happened to be reading the sixth chapter of Romans, and He drew my attention to the eleventh verse: "Likewise reckon ye also yourselves to be dead indeed unto sin, but alive unto God through Jesus Christ our Lord" (Romans 6:11 KJV).

Suddenly, the word *reckon* lit up and flashed on the page like a neon sign. Although I had read this chapter countless times and even had it memorized, I had never noticed this word or thought about its meaning. I did not realize it yet, but the Lord was raising an issue. Over the years I had constructed a spiritual list of "holy things to do" and "unholy things to avoid." I was diligent to keep my list up every day, and I felt pretty good about myself.

Instead of a pat on the back for approval, however, I got the feeling that there was something very wrong with my holiness program. With that feeling came the sudden awareness that, while I was busy keeping my holiness checklist, I had also begun considering myself holier than those who were not keeping checklists that were as long or as robust as mine.

It is amazing how the Spirit of the Lord brings things to the surface. I was shocked to realize that while I had been sincerely striving to stay steady on my holiness course, I had unwittingly developed spiritual pride. My holiness program was seriously flawed, and now I had a problem on my hands; pride, after all, is no small sin!

The Lord encouraged me with these words: *Georgian, why don't you just do what My written instruction says and simply reckon yourself dead to sin and alive to Me?*

"Lord, I'm so sorry," I objected, "but this is the first time that I have realized what You require from me. Now that I understand that holiness comes through reckoning, I will do it. Please let me practice and then I'll get really good at it. Besides that, Lord, You just showed me that I have pride. I need time to deal with this sin before I can confidently say that I'm dead to it."

It is amazing how we argue with the Lord, and yet He remains patient and keeps giving us another chance.

Do it now, Georgian, He said. *Don't delay any longer, agree with what I've declared in the Word for you.*

Everything inside me wanted to respond in obedience to the Lord at that moment, but I simply could not see how I could acknowledge something so monumental. I needed time to improve, time to practice being dead to sin.

The Lord was not at all interested in my predicament; He waited for my obedient response.

Exasperated, I cried out, "On the basis of what, Lord? How can I say that I am something that I'm not, or that I have something that I haven't taken the time to obtain? You just exposed the really big sin of spiritual pride in my life, and I'll gladly deal with it, but please give me time to reckon it done."

I had several Bible translations with me, and the Lord kindly answered again by asking me to grab my New American Standard Bible and turn to find Romans 8:3. That is where I read that what the Law could not do, *God did*.

> For what the Law could not do, weak as it was through the flesh, God did: sending His own Son in the likeness of sinful flesh and as an offering for sin, He condemned sin in the flesh, so that the requirement of the Law might be fulfilled in us, who do not walk according to the flesh but according to the Spirit.
>
> Romans 8:3–4

When I saw the phrase *God did* under the spotlight of His attention, the words exploded in my spirit like an atomic bomb. *God did* what the Law could not do. *God did* it by sending Jesus to meet the requirements of His Law in us.

Receive My glorious gift, Georgian, He said. *Open it up and let this powerful revelation take over. I paid for you to have it with My body and blood; consume it and let it consume you. Go ahead, reckon it on the basis of My finished work. Reckon yourself dead to sin and alive to Me. What you need to do now is nurture this revelation.*

This powerful visit from Jesus took place on the very first day of a brand-new chapter in my life. All sorts of human emotions tried to flood my soul, but Jesus was more interested in my biblical foundation. Quitting a successful band meant losing our income, and we had just said goodbye to all of our dearest friends and our community. But the Lord wanted me to step into the *now* of what Christ accomplished on my behalf and, ultimately, set me free from performance and striving.

A Hug from God as Father

Winnie and I decided to leave town and go far away, somewhere that we had never been before. We needed to be able to rest and wait before the Lord for clearer instructions. A friend provided inexpensive missionary housing for us in London, and that is where we went.

Yana was only six months old, and spending time together as a family in our little flat was something that we had not been able to do very much of before. We took some time to compose music and be creative, but mostly we just rested. In fact, this was the first real rest that either one of us could remember taking.

It was during this time of refreshing that the Lord showed up for another important visit, and this time, He came to me as my *Father*.

He said, *Georgian, I'm your Master, and you've served Me well. That's good. I'm your God, and you've worshiped Me beautifully and from your heart; that's very good, too. I've been your General, and you've been a good soldier; you take orders well. That's all good, and we'll keep all of that.*

He continued, *But now, Georgian, I want you to know Me as your Father.*

With that last sentence, I froze. I had no idea what to do with a father. I felt extremely awkward.

The Lord continued, *Georgian, the problem is that you always need to do something. You've stepped in and filled a lot of roles. You do a great job; there's nothing wrong with that in and of itself, but you don't seem to understand being My son. Georgian, you must understand that I'm not only your Savior, but I'm also your Father.*

I sat completely still.

Georgian, you cannot do anything to become My son. Fathers and mothers make their sons and daughters; children don't make themselves for their parents. Spiritually, it's the same way. Through Jesus, you became My son. When you accepted My Son's sacrifice, you became born again. You were born from Me. I gave you a brand-new life and a new heart. Your new existence and your identity now come from Me. I'm pleased with you from the start because I made you, and you are Mine.

I was still silent.

He said, *Georgian, since you're so into doing something, how about a hug?*

When I first got saved and saw the Lord on His throne in heaven, I knew that He was enormous. I did not know how a hug could be possible.

"But, God," I said, "You are huge! How can I hug You?"

He said to me, *Don't worry, I'll size down. Just reach out and hug Me.*

I was feeling Him drawing closer, but I could not see Him, and I could not connect with how I would hug Him.

He then told me to grab the pillow next to me and hug it. *That will help you,* He explained.

Having a pillow provided something physical, and it relaxed me enough to step into hugging the Father. As I started hugging, I could sense my arms going around His neck and then His arms embracing me and squeezing me tight. All of a sudden, something happened. All of my fears and insecurities got squeezed right out of me. *Whoosh!* In that moment, in the absence of all of those things that held me back, all I could feel was pure love. There was so much love I felt as if I were swimming in it.

The Lord said, *Do you feel My Father's love for you? You can't increase it, Georgian. I'm infusing you with My love for you as My son. You can't manipulate that. You can't do any-thing to increase it. You also can't decrease it, stop it or mini-mize it. All you can do is just receive it.*

His love for me was not connected to anything that I had done or anything that I would or would not do. It shifted my self-image.

I sobbed for hours into that pillow.

Then, sitting there, drying my eyes, I wondered how this revelation took more than ten years to discover from that moment when I had first met Him.

Even though I had read my Bible thoroughly, the verses pointing to God as my Father had never registered in my mind. Lacking a relationship with my earthly dad, those Scriptures had just passed me by, for I had no framework or context for them. Even when Jesus spoke from the perspective of a Son, I could not comprehend any of it.

Was I saved and going to heaven? Yes.

Was I able to enjoy time in His presence, worship Him and feel His love? Yes.

Was I serving the Lord and ministering to His people? Yes.

The truth is, if I died the moment after I became born again, I would have gone straight to heaven to be His child forever. From God's point of view, because I had accepted His Son, Jesus, as my Savior, I was not only saved, but also accepted in His sonship. All that being true, the Lord wanted more. He wanted me to live out the full measure of my identity as a son while here on earth, too.

You Are God's Child!

Romans 8:15–16 in the Passion Translation describes perfectly how God met me as "Beloved Father."

And you did not receive the "spirit of religious duty," leading you back into the fear of never being good enough. But you have received the "Spirit of full acceptance," enfolding you into the family of God. And you will never feel orphaned, for as he rises up within us, our spirits join him in saying the words of tender affection, "Beloved Father!" For the Holy Spirit makes God's fatherhood real to us as he whispers into our innermost being, "You are God's beloved child!"

Romans 8:15–16 TPT

This is how God wants to meet you, too. Let Him be your Dad and wrap you in His love embrace.

4

Jesus to the Core

When Yana was learning how to walk, Winnie and I cheered her along as she attempted to pull herself up and stand on her two little feet. Even though she took her fair share of tumbles, none of that mattered to us for we knew that our sweet little girl would soon be able to gain her balance.

With each new step that she took, I understood what the Lord was speaking to me. Up until recently, I had lived like an orphan. The encounter that left me sobbing into my pillow opened a new door for me. I was now learning to walk as a son greatly loved by the Father.

The Lord knew that it would take time for me to grasp the fullness of what had happened. The fact that He loves me just as He loves His Son laid the foundation that forever altered my understanding of my relationship with Him. He encouraged me continually, and I started to relax in sonship and trust.

The two grand revelations that He had given me were now playing on a continuous loop inside of my spirit:

1. "Reckon yourself dead to sin and alive to God in Christ; what the law could not do, *God did*."
2. "You are My son forever, and I will always love you fully. There is nothing that you can do to increase or diminish My fatherly love for you."

Even though fears and insecurities would try to come back, they could never go deep inside me and stay. As a son in His arms, I understood that I no longer faced challenges alone. With a big, big Dad on my side who reminded me continually to trust Him, I learned to cast my mounting cares on Him; fears could no longer get me the way they used to.

As I came to Him daily for His fatherly affection, I began to accept the fact that He wanted to enjoy me, too—as a son. By stepping into sonship, I was making my way into wholeness. I found myself being infused with childlike joy as He taught me to take delight in Him.

It began to dawn on me that the "wineskin change" that I had anticipated did not have anything to do with some sort of new worship music or new band. The Holy Spirit was bringing to light the truth about my new identity and the essence of my new birth. The upgrade and expansion of faith that I had cried out for in war-torn Uganda could come only as the finished work of His crucified Son came clearly into focus. This revelation was the new wine that the Lord wanted to give me. Yet, to be able to contain it, I first had to become a son.

Was it a process? Yes, His Word was being opened up to me in a fresh new way and my mind was being renewed daily. A glorious world of discovery was set before me. He wanted to show me what I had been missing. While I had always understood that Jesus offered Himself as a sacrifice for my sins, I had missed the fact that when He died on the cross, something happened to me—I died, too.

The Fall of Humanity and God's Solution

To grasp the full magnitude of what Christ accomplished, I began by looking at the severity of what happened during humanity's Fall. When the Lord placed Adam and Eve in the Garden, He told them that they could eat from any tree except from the Tree of Knowledge of Good and Evil. Why? Because eating from that tree would cause them to die (cease to exist) spiritually (to God): "But of the tree of the knowledge of good and evil and blessing and calamity you shall not eat, *for in the day that you eat of it you shall surely die*" (Genesis 2:17 AMPC, emphasis added).

Satan used the serpent to question Adam and Eve about what God had said. He twisted God's warning: "You will not surely die. . . . For God knows that when you eat of it your eyes will be opened, and you will be like God, knowing good and evil" (Genesis 3:4–5 NIV1984).

The truth is, God had already created Adam and Eve to be like Himself, yet without the devastating effects of the knowledge of good and evil: "God said, 'Let us make mankind in our image, to be like us'" (Genesis 1:26 ISV).

God had already blessed them to be fruitful, multiply and subdue the earth. When they bit into the lie of the deceiver, however, they became permanently separated from God. The Supplanter succeeded in ruining the plan of God for Adam and Eve and their offspring to rule the earth under God's leadership. Thus, they forfeited their authority and divine inheritance into the hands of the enemy.

At that point, Adam and Eve's existence became distorted by the deception that they could exist independently from God. Corruption entered in; their innocence was gone. Instead of existing independently from God, as the deceiver had suggested, they now found themselves bitterly estranged from Him.

That is the horror of it all; the collateral damage of spiritual death was instant. Adam and Eve did not slowly become corrupt; it went viral immediately. The delusion corrupted their minds and their souls, and their bodies began to decay. Murder manifested itself as their firstborn son, Cain, killed his younger brother, Abel. In the loins of Adam, the seed of humanity in its entirety was fully corrupted. We had now become a race of sinners, rotten to the core by birth and by nature.

Adam and Eve were ashamed and remorseful, and God in His mercy forgave them. But forgiveness alone was not enough to cure the problem, for they had become trafficked as slaves to the dark forces of sin, evil and death.

In their shame, Adam and Eve covered themselves with fig leaves. The leaves were not sufficient, however, and the Lord slaughtered an innocent animal to provide their covering. This act showed that the shedding of blood was the price for redemption. While the animal skins offered a temporary outward solution, it would ultimately take the blood of the Lamb to remedy humanity's fallen condition.

When the time was right, the Father sent His perfect Son, Jesus, who shed His own blood. He did this not only to wash away our sins, but also to cure us from our old nature, which was corrupt to the core, and to set us free from the curse of the Law and our efforts to exist independently from God: "Christ redeemed us from that self-defeating, cursed life by absorbing it completely into himself" (Galatians 3:13 MSG).

He became a curse on the tree, and then He absorbed that curse and dissolved it. You could say, "He killed everything that was killing us."

All That Is Included with Salvation

I was learning more and more that our new birth is absolutely miraculous. The moment that we say yes to Jesus as Savior we become born again, a beautiful new creation with a brand-new spirit. When Jesus died on the cross, He not only forgave our sins, He also baptized us into His death in order to destroy the controlling power of sin in our lives: "Do you not know that all of us who have been *baptized into Christ Jesus have been baptized into His death?*" (Romans 6:3, emphasis added). In this verse, the apostle Paul used the Greek word *baptizō* to explain what happens to us. *Baptizō* is not just a religious word as it is perceived today: It was a common word used in recipes.

Theologian James Montgomery Boice explains this.

Of all the texts that might be cited from antiquity, the one that gives the greatest clarity to this issue is a text from a Greek poet and physician, Nicander, who lived about 200 BC. In a recipe for making pickles he used both words. Nicander said that the vegetable should first be dipped (*baptō*) in boiling water and then baptized (*baptizō*) in the vinegar solution. Both had to do with immersing the vegetable in the solution. But the first was temporary, while the other, the operation of baptizing the vegetable, produced a permanent change. The sacrament of baptism points to our identification with Christ by faith.[1]

1. James Montgomery Boice, *Foundations of the Christian Faith* (Downers Grove, Ill.: InterVarsity, 2019), 615.

Paul was making the meaning clear. Baptism into Christ's death brings permanent change.

Growing up in Bulgaria, we grew our own vegetables and pickled as much as we could just to have enough to eat during our winters. I certainly understood pickling. During my summer visits to my grandma's house I would watch her take a whole bunch of cucumbers and immerse them into a hot solution with salt, vinegar, dill and other spices. In time, they turned into something altogether new: my favorite pickles. Everything about them had changed. They no longer tasted like cucumbers. The bacteria that would have caused them to spoil were destroyed, and we could enjoy our pickles all year long.

Though I never knew exactly how Grandma changed her cucumbers into pickles, there is one thing that I can tell you to this day: I have never seen someone take a pickle and turn it back into a cucumber. The change is permanent and irreversible.

The apostle Paul wrote that "*our old self was crucified with Him*, in order that our body of sin might be done away with, so that we would no longer be slaves to sin; for he who has died is freed from sin" (Romans 6:6–7, emphasis added). This means that anyone who is born again becomes "a new being; the old is gone, the new has come" (2 Corinthians 5:17 GNT).

Jesus died so that we could be with Him eternally. This is the fountainhead of absolute peace and joy. Yet there is even more! When we are baptized into Christ's death, He single-handedly brings about a permanent change. He not only forgives our sins and sets us free from shame and condemnation, He also sets us free from our corrupt nature and the world of sin that enslaved us.

What Jesus Did for You

Ezekiel prophesied the dramatic change that would come at the cross.

> "I'll give you a new heart, put a new spirit in you. I'll remove the stone heart from your body and replace it with a heart that's God-willed, not self-willed. I'll put my Spirit in you and make it possible for you to do what I tell you and live by my commands."
>
> Ezekiel 36:26 MSG

Colossians describes the fulfillment of this prophecy another way. On the cross, Christ performed a spiritual circumcision by cutting away that rotten nature that once ruled us in our core.

> In Him also you were circumcised with a circumcision not made with hands, but in a [spiritual] circumcision [performed by] Christ by stripping off the body of the flesh (the whole corrupt, carnal nature with its passions and lusts).
>
> Colossians 2:11 AMPC

When we accept Jesus as our Savior, we step into sweet eternal union with Him. This is the extraordinary gift of His grace. When I finally believed it, cascading joy exploded within me.

This does not mean we behave perfectly going forward, and by no means am I saying that we are sinless. But because we are now in an intimate faith-trust relationship with the Lord, He guides us and course-corrects us through His Word and the indwelling Holy Spirit. Sin is now an external entity, an external force that lures by temptation. It no longer has dominion over us; Jesus is our Master and we are now under His authority and grace. He gives us the power to resist that external force.

Today, many Christian and even some secular sources proclaim that the number-one enemy of humanity is the *ego* or the *self*—if you fail to control *it* properly, *it* will act up against your relationships, your family, your boss, your company, your position—and ultimately *it* will betray you.

The Gospel, however, is not about improving the *I*, the *self*, the *ego*. It is about this: "*Not I, but Christ.*"

> For I through the law am dead to the law, that I might live unto God. I am crucified with Christ: nevertheless I live; yet *not I, but Christ* liveth in me: and the life which I now live in the flesh I live by the faith of the Son of God, who loved me, and gave himself for me.
>
> Galatians 2:19–20 AKJV, emphasis added

Not a single one of us can free ourselves from that *old identity*; only Jesus can. He came to crucify the "I" on the cross, and to destroy the lie of the independent self-existence (ego) that the devil and world system uses to enslave us.

That is why it is essential that we never reduce or lose sight of the magnitude of what Christ our Redeemer accomplished on the cross. His sacrifice was not solely to forgive our sins and secure our access into heaven: He makes us brand new. If we were to believe that Jesus covers over our rottenness and allows the poison of the serpent to remain inside of us until we finally make it to heaven, we would be denying the fullness and grandeur of His death and resurrection.

Adam Clarke, a brilliant eighteenth-century Wesleyan theologian, put it this way: "If we are waiting for our physical death to free us once and for all from the power of sin, then we have just crowned death as our savior and not the Lord Jesus Christ."

Jesus sets us free. What a great victory! It is intoxicating. We are no longer sinners, rotten to the core—in Christ we are now saints, with Jesus to the core. Greater is He that is in us than he that is in the world! (see 1 John 4:4).

Your License to Rejoice

When Paul exhorted the believers of the first European church that he and Silas planted to "rejoice in the Lord always," he repeated it: "Again I will say rejoice" (Philippians 4:4). The apostle to the non-Jewish world was writing from prison while awaiting execution, and he was modeling the secret for a victorious Christian life.

Jesus the Master is now inside of us, and our rejoicing is a mandate. Rejoicing should be like breathing, especially through difficulties and trials, for His joy is our strength.

This is how the Lord discipled me as a young believer. *I've set you free, Georgian, so honor Me with your joyful response. Live this life of freedom that I gave to you. Remember to rejoice in Me; serve Me with joy and live it to the fullest.*

We have been authorized and commissioned to rejoice. Joy is heaven's serious business, after all. Perhaps you have been convinced to let your joy license expire? Well, have it back, my friend! You have full permission to rejoice in Him again and again and again.

The revelation of what He did for us at the cross launches us into His joy, and His joy is the secret weapon of every believer. By serving Him with joy and gladness of heart, the joy that is in Him shields us from the enemy's fiery darts of sorrow and depression. This joy not only strengthens us, it also gives us courage, making us bold and brave.

5

Faith inside Christ

I n the summer of 1989, the Lord spoke to me very clearly:
*Georgian, I want you to get ready. You are about to go home
to Bulgaria, and you will be able to see your family and all
of your old friends.*

Since my escape through the Iron Curtain in 1972, I never
believed that I would be able to return to Bulgaria. I knew full
well that the Communists would arrest me on the spot and send
me straight to prison if I were found inside their borders. But
the Lord was very clear about the fact that I was going home,
and while I had no idea how this was going to work, He gave
me peace. Somehow, Winnie and I knew that everything was
going to be okay, and I had no fear.

In the months that followed, I sent newsletters to my American
friends explaining that the Lord told me I was going home for
the first time since my escape.

One of my friends was so excited that he sent me a generous
donation, and with that I purchased my ticket to Bulgaria. My

flight was scheduled for the first week in March—by then the harshest winter months would be over.

That November, East Berlin's Communist party began dismantling the Berlin Wall. There was no way that I could have known it, but that event would lead to the collapse of the Iron Curtain. In the months ahead, riots and unrest began to spread throughout Eastern Europe.

On Christmas Day, the news came that Communism was falling. Romania's dictator, Nicolae Ceauşescu, and his wife, Elena, were taken outside and shot by a firing squad. The Romanian people were revolting in the streets; they had had enough of his tyranny and cruelty. I watched the news for ten hours straight; I could not get enough. Every half hour, as the news was cycled over and over again, the sound bite that "the Antichrist died on Christmas Day" was played.

The general secretary of the Bulgarian Communist Party, dictator Tudor Zhivkov, was arrested just weeks later. In February, the Communists officially relinquished their power.

Never dreaming that their grip on Bulgaria would come to an end, I walked around in shock and awe for days. Communism had collapsed. The unthinkable had happened, and the Lord had me ready. My tickets had already been purchased, and I would be home in just a few weeks.

Now that it was safe to take Winnie and Yana, I got them tickets to fly with me. Winnie's sister, Jeri, came with us, too. We stopped over in Holland, where Brother Andrew's office (Brother Andrew known, of course, as "God's Smuggler" for his courage in taking Bibles into Communist countries) loaded us with boxes of Bulgarian Bibles.

Throughout the years I had stayed in touch with my mother. I sent her letters, usually with a Polaroid picture enclosed to share with her a glimpse of her extended family and our life in the United States. During the holidays I would call her. Of course, the Communists read all of our mail and listened to our phone conversations. We had to be cryptic. If I would say something that the Communists did not like, then my letter would never arrive in her mailbox.

That summer, I wrote letting her know that I would be coming home, and to help spread the word. Once my flight was booked, I sent her the details.

When we landed at the airport in Sofia, my family was there to greet us—my mother, my grandmother and, to my amazement, on the other side of the arrival doors stood my father with his new family. They were so happy to meet Winnie and Yana. What a magnificent reunion we all had! None of us thought that we would ever see each other again, and we were elated. Our hearts were bursting as we enjoyed the most beautiful family moments.

Everywhere we went, people were euphoric. Revolution was in the streets. I found all of my old rock-and-roll friends and joined them at parties. Being able to share my faith in Jesus with them was my biggest delight. That week I gave away Brother Andrew's Bibles to grateful pastors who pleaded with me for more.

I began calling Bible societies throughout Europe. This was March and my hope was to distribute Bibles on May 24 to celebrate Bulgaria's one-thousand-year anniversary as a Christian nation. Those tyrants who had tried to outlaw God were now stripped of their power; Christianity was here to stay. We wanted publicly to honor the Lord, who had caused the underground Church to triumph in spite of persecution.

The German Bible Society told me they could do it, but they would need at least six months to print my order. Word got out that I was calling around, and the Lord divinely connected me with someone in Sweden who had a full set of printing plates for the Bulgarian Bible in his possession. The plates had been smuggled to safety when Communism began gaining power. He said he was very glad to connect with me. "I've heard of you," he said. "You are the persistent Bulgarian. The Bible Societies are all talking about you. I believe in miracles. Quick, go raise the money and we will meet this crazy deadline of yours."

On my return to the United States, I was able to appear on CBN's *The 700 Club*, where I made an appeal. Pat Robertson generously gave me $15,000. I immediately called Sweden to start the printing presses. With the help of a few other ministries, even more funds were raised, and I called again to increase my order. Our Swedish friends were able to make the deadline and, with great joy, we were able to hand out more than forty thousand Bibles on that special anniversary date. Everyone went wild as we distributed the Bibles. Pastors were crying; some even kissed my hands out of gratitude. It was an exuberant time, and the memory of it is permanently etched into my heart and mind. To this day, many of those pastors are my friends. They keep those Bibles as a treasure.

In June, Bulgaria held its first democratic election. During this critical period, I travelled back and forth between the United States and Bulgaria as frequently as I could.

Lisa Osteen, a daughter of John Osteen, the founding pastor of Lakewood Church in Houston, Texas, had been a Silverwind fan. As a result, I found myself invited to sing a few songs and give my testimony at her father's church. As I played my violin and spoke to the large audience, the Holy Spirit fell on the people.

With that, Pastor John pulled me to the side and asked if I would be willing to preach a message right then and there.

I said, "Absolutely!"

He said, "Take it until nine o'clock. Go for it!"

This was during an evening service with almost ten thousand people in attendance. Toward the end of my message, I shared about what was happening in Bulgaria. Then the Holy Spirit emboldened me.

I turned to Pastor John, asking him, "Pastor, Bulgaria is wide open to the Gospel right now. Will you come and help me raise leaders?"

Pastor John jumped up and responded in front of everyone. "I've been invited to Bulgaria several times before but never made it there. Now I'm sensing that this is the right invitation from the right messenger. I can feel the anointing, so yes, Georgian, I'm going to Bulgaria with you!"

He made plans for his son Justin and me to go ahead of him to Bulgaria so that we could get things rolling. We organized everything. The day was approaching for our nationwide gathering of pastors and leaders.

We had rented a huge facility and blasted the word across Bulgaria. This was a critical time for the nation. I knew that Pastor John would be able to make a significant impact on the Christian leaders. For years, they had had to hide their activities, going underground. They were all extra good at being invisible. But this was a new season. It was time for them to rise up and stand out as leaders. The souls of Bulgaria were ripe for the harvest, and these pastors needed to be built up and strengthened in the Lord.

God's Faith Is Restful

Our event was held in an old opera house in Varna, a beautiful Black Sea resort city. It was our first night, and the building was packed with more than a thousand Bulgarian pastors and core ministry leaders. They came from all over the nation and from every denomination. At this time, Communism maintained a stronghold on certain pockets of the country. Because Varna was a popular resort destination for the Russian Soviet leaders, the Communist authorities of the city were still powerful there. Once they saw what was happening that first night, they objected fiercely and made plans to shut us down.

Later that night, the police began threatening us. By morning we received the news that they were shutting us down for good; our evening service was now officially cancelled. It felt as if all hell had broken loose.

Immediately I began calling my friends in the capital city of Sofia, most of whom were heavily connected with radio and television. Being a known rock-and-roll personality, I could create a media stir. The new democratic leadership that was forming also knew me; in their eyes I was a "rebel hero" because of my escape, and they liked that.

One after the other I continued making phone calls reaching out to everyone and anyone who had the power to help. My goal was to pull on every string that I could think of.

By lunchtime, Pastor John spoke to me. "You are letting yourself get too worried. Don't stress. It's all going to work out." He began to talk to me about faith, "You know, Georgian, true faith is very restful."

He began to share with me that Houston, being a big oil city, was hit extremely hard by the energy crisis during the '70s. It was a tough time for their congregation and everyone in the community. Yet, even though the economy was devastated, God told him at that time to build a new church building.

The Lord instructed him to share this vision with the people and take an offering. Not only was the economy of Houston depressed, it was also Christmas season, which, as a rule, is not the best time to take an offering. To his joy and amazement, the entire amount of money needed for the building came that very day through love gifts and pledges.

"Georgian, that just goes to show you that when God says something will happen, it will happen, no matter the economy or the circumstances." He continued to encourage me, but I still struggled under the stress of it. As the host for this unprecedented national event, I felt responsible to fix everything, and that burden was weighing me down.

"I'm glad that you're thinking like that, Pastor John," I said, "but you have no idea what's going on outside in the city. It's a war. Communists hate Christians. We've pushed their buttons, and the evil powers controlling them are determined to shut us down. They are pulling out all the stops."

By midafternoon, he could still hear me calling all my friends and contacts in Sofia, urging them to help overturn the decision made by the local authorities. Pastor John was getting ready to take a nap, and he called out to me from the room we shared in the apartment suite where all of us were staying, "Hey, Georgian, it's going to be okay, come on. It's time to rest before tonight's service. Lie down and take a break."

"Okay," I muttered.

Feeling there was little choice, I made myself lie down, even though I was completely at wits' end. Staring at the ceiling while my mind raced in a million directions, I noticed all of a sudden that his breathing had changed; he had fallen asleep. Something began to happen as I lay there listening. It felt as though a blanket came over me. The peace that he carried, that mantle of restful faith that he was talking to me about, came over me, and everything changed. Instantly it hit me; God is the one who put these meetings together. Somehow, deep inside, I felt that everything was going to be okay.

Eventually I got up. As I stared out at the beautiful Black Sea from the balcony window, the Lord continued ministering to me. How grateful I was for Pastor Osteen's wisdom and mentoring. He saw that I had taken all of the responsibility for the leadership conference onto my own shoulders instead of giving my burdens to the Lord. In so doing, I had let myself become filled with stress and anxiety, and had lost my joy. Pastor John demonstrated Christ to me that afternoon, and by his fatherly help I was able to step back into the rest of God where I belonged. Jesus, the Ruler over the universe, would take care of those Communists and the dark forces antagonizing us.

Sure enough, everything switched to our favor. We were able to continue our meetings as planned without any resistance for the rest of that weekend. The Lord worked it all out, and the pastors and leaders were strengthened and blessed.

The greatest impact that the Varna event had on me personally was the revelation that God's faith is restful. The powerful impartation that I received from Pastor Osteen left me longing to know more.

The Nature of Faith

I began searching the Scriptures to explore the nature of faith. The Bible tells us that without faith, it is impossible to please God (see Hebrews 11:6). I aimed always to please Him, but now I realized that I had crossed over a line. Once again I was striving to find favor in the Lord's eyes. I had fallen into the old pattern of self-effort.

But I could not help wondering how faith works. Reflecting back, I considered how I was born into an antichrist system and indoctrinated as an atheist. If faith is what it takes to believe, and if faith is what it takes to please God, then it seems I would have never stood a chance.

As I thought about my salvation journey in this light, I began to marvel at how it had been accomplished. When those Jesus People spotted me, I can imagine that they prayed, "Oh, Lord, what do we do with this wild rock-and-roll Bulgarian atheist?" But because they felt God's love toward me, they said, "You know what? Jesus loves you. He died for you. He believes in you, Georgian."

Their genuine fellowship began chipping away at the atheist inside me. Faith kept rising from their hearts as they patiently spent time with me, causing me finally to ask out loud, "God, do You exist?"

Pastor John Osteen's reaction further demonstrated to me that the spirit of true faith does not incite anxiety, but rests confidently in God's ability. I remembered the Lord's warning in Hebrews: "Let it then be our earnest endeavour to be admitted to that rest, so that no one may perish through following the same example of unbelief" (Hebrews 4:11 WNT).

I had begun living my new life by the power of the Spirit. How could I now try to finish living it by my own efforts? The apostle Paul questioned the Galatian church about this, and the same was being asked of me (see Galatians 3:3).

But something else was becoming clear in all of this. I saw now that it was really Jesus pursuing me all along: "So then faith comes by hearing, and hearing by the word of God" (Romans 10:17 NKJV).

While human faith is based on performance, God's saving faith is wrapped up in Jesus and His work on the cross. The faith that it takes to believe comes to us as a pure love gift: "For it is by God's grace that you have been saved through faith. It is not the result of your own efforts, but God's gift, so that no one can boast about it (Ephesians 2:8–9 GNT). The faith that saves us comes by God's grace. Once we receive it, it empowers us to believe. As the Bible says, with the heart we believe, and with the mouth we confess.

The well-known line about faith in the book of Hebrews was making more sense to me: "Now faith is the *substance* of things hoped for, the evidence of things not seen" (Hebrews 11:1 KJV, emphasis added).

When I asked God that searching question about His existence those years ago, something came upon me; it was a substance of sorts, evidence. His presence was like a canopy tangibly covering me. Suddenly I knew that there was a God. In an instant it had all made sense.

The Greek word *hypostasis* (*Strong's* G5287) used in Hebrews defining faith as a "substance" is the same word used to describe Jesus as the radiance of God's glory and the exact representation of His "nature" (Hebrews 1:3 BSB). As Jesus reveals the nature of the Father, faith reveals the Father's heart and will for us, and empowers us to believe. Faith is wrapped up in Christ Himself, and He activates faith in our hearts.

Paul's letter to the Galatians gave me something further to ponder in this regard: "Now that *faith* has come, we are no longer under a tutor" (Galatians 3:25, emphasis added). I found that a couple of lesser-known translations actually capitalize the word *faith*: "Now that the Faith is come. . . ."[1]

I wondered why they did that, and was interested to see that the Living Bible actually uses the word *Christ* instead of *faith* in this verse: "Now that *Christ* has come, we don't need those

---

1. Helen Barrett Montgomery, *The Centenary Translation of the New Testament* (Texarkana, Tex.: American Baptist Publication Society, 1924). See also J.W.C. Wand, D.D., *The New Testament Letters, Prefaced and Paraphrased by J.W.C. Wand, D.D.* (Melbourne: Oxford University Press, 1944).

laws any longer to guard us and lead us to him" (emphasis added).

Just as Jesus is our righteousness, our wisdom and our redemption, we can also say that He is our faith.

In a further discovery, I found that Habakkuk 2:4 tells us that "the just shall live by his faith" (NKJV). Commentators generally agree that this refers to each person's own faith and trust in the righteousness of Jesus. Certain translations of a verse in Hebrews, however, give us an interesting insight that the just live by *God's* faith, or by the faithfulness of the Son of God. The writer of Hebrews quotes Habakkuk while explaining Christ's eternal sacrifice: "But the righteous one shall live by my faith" (Hebrews 10:38 ARAMAIC BIBLE IN PLAIN ENGLISH); and "My righteous ones will live from my faith" (TPT).

When Jesus embraced our sinfulness on the cross, He trusted the Father completely. He was about to become sin and die in our curses and separation from God. Mind you, this was not a dress rehearsal. Jesus remained faithful to the Father's plan, being confident in His ability to resurrect Him.

When the soldiers came to arrest Him, Jesus asked, "Who is it you want?"

They replied, "Jesus of Nazareth."

When Jesus said, "I am He," all of the soldiers drew back and fell to the ground. At any moment He could have easily called a squadron of angels to deliver Him. Earlier in the Garden of Gethsemane, however, He had yielded to His Father: "Not My will, but Your will be done."

Our salvation comes through Jesus' willingness to embrace the cross while trusting that He would be raised up from the dead. This divine trust, this faith of Christ, made the way for our salvation and empowers us to live as His new creation. The apostle Paul powerfully declared, "I am crucified with Christ:

nevertheless I live; yet not I, but Christ liveth in me: and the life which I now live in the flesh I live by the faith of the Son of God, who loved me, and gave himself for me" (Galatians 2:20 KJV).

Some Bible translators suggest the Greek article *tou* (*Strong's* G3588) in this verse could be translated to say that "we live by faith *in the* Son of God." Other translators, as I have mentioned, point out that we actually "live *by the* faith of the Son of God." My own Bulgarian Bible when translated into English says it this way: "The life I live, I live by the faith that is in the Son of God." I read this as saying that the faith we live by is an integral part of who He is. That helps us understand the proper meaning of this verse and avoid misinterpreting its core message: "not I, but Christ."

Years after this, Winnie and I gathered together a team of scholars, funding a first-of-its-kind Bulgarian Interlinear Bible project. We enjoyed direct access to a team of leading Bible scholars, as well as philologists and linguists whose field of expertise is ancient Greek. They advised me that both "in" and "of" are included in the meaning of this Greek word *tou*, and they further explained that "the faith of the Son of God" is the best way to translate this verse.

Bottom line, Christianity is not about trying to do something for God by our own efforts or willpower. It is Christ who comes to live in us by His Spirit when He births us anew. Energized by love, we start our faith journey united with Him— believing that together we can move mountains and heal the sick. We are not manufacturing faith on our own, but, rather, we are responding to His voice in trust as He speaks His Word in our hearts.

This new understanding of faith was a revelation—but I was to learn that it was only part of the revelation that God had for me. There was more to come.

Building Your Faith

Do you see why reading, studying and meditating on the Word is so vital? It centers us in His will, and, in so doing, we experience His joy and pleasure: "May the words of my mouth and the meditation of my heart be pleasing to you, O Lord, my rock and my redeemer" (Psalm 19:14 NLT). It is essential that in addition to meditating on the Word, we also read it out loud, remembering that faith comes by hearing.

By verbalizing the Word, we obtain His precious promises. We prophesy, heal the sick, work miracles and remove obstacles: "Truly, I say to you, whoever *says* to this mountain, 'Be taken up and thrown into the sea,' and does not doubt in his heart, but believes that what he *says* will come to pass, it will be done for him" (Mark 11:23 ESV, emphasis added).

I encourage you to hear Him saying, *I am the Author and the Finisher of your faith* (see Hebrews 12:2 KJV), *and I will not leave you on your own. I am always with you.*

This type of relational faith always produces results because our God of wonders is intimately involved with us, making our lives of faith both restful and joyous: "Whom having not seen, you love; in whom, though now you see him not, yet believing, you rejoice with joy unspeakable and full of glory" (1 Peter 1:8 KJV2000).

6
Performance-Free Grace

I am forever grateful for the foundation of faith that the Lord laid in my heart. Yet there was more to come. The Lord also wanted to teach me about His grace, for His faith and grace go together hand in hand. To share this part of my journey with you, I need to go back in time.

When Winnie and I left Silverwind in 1985, even though we stepped out in obedience, our excitement was short-lived. I wish that I could say that our next chapter in life was smooth like silk, but that was not the case. We had given up our steady income and were starting over from scratch. The grace of God kept us from sinking. Without the backing of a public relations machine or support system such as we had been used to, we felt completely alone.

In time and with some twists and turns along the way, the Lord helped me find my new place in ministry. Churches invited me to come and share my testimony with their congregations, and missionary organizations called on me to teach their students. I also had the opportunity to create worship and ministry resources while helping develop a youth program with some pastor friends. Once the Iron Curtain collapsed, my missionary work exploded. I found myself travelling back and forth to Bulgaria at least five times a year. Through the help of my pastor here in America, we were able to create a leadership program for all of our Bulgarian pastors who had been worn down by the Communists. They needed fresh vision and strength to handle the new harvest that was upon them. It was an exciting yet busy time; we were filled with hope as we dedicated ourselves to rebuilding Bulgaria's new future in Christ.

When we had first moved to Tacoma, Washington, Winnie and I began attending a church associated with the Word of Faith movement. Even though it was completely out of our paradigm, the faith message inspired me.

Winnie, however, eventually stopped going to church, and soon after, she quit the ministry altogether. As her husband, I sort of understood her decision but did not know how to help her. The faith message that I had embraced fully had become difficult for Winnie. For some reason she felt nothing but pressure to believe and perform, and when she tried to read her Bible, she just felt condemned.

Our marriage slowly began to deteriorate, and in time we were more like two roommates living together. I came dangerously close to considering divorce as an option but was just too embarrassed to go through with it. While I worked hard to stay connected to ministry, I could not preach the new revelations that the Lord had given me because our failing marriage was continually staring me in the face and wearing me down.

One day I confided in a very dear pastor friend from Florida. As I told him about my marital troubles, he kindly challenged me to pray for Winnie thirty minutes every day. It was too painful to explain that I had already given up praying for my wife and for our marriage, but since I could not say no to my friend, I promised him that I would.

During my first attempt, I realized that I had absolutely no words to pray with. Then the thought came to pray in tongues instead.

> The Holy Spirit helps us in our weakness. For example, we don't know what God wants us to pray for. But the Holy Spirit prays for us with groanings that cannot be expressed in words. And the Father who knows all hearts knows what the Spirit is saying, for the Spirit pleads for us believers in harmony with God's own will.
>
> Romans 8:26–27 NLT

After a few days and weeks of praying in the Holy Ghost, springs of hope began to bubble up in my heart again, and in the months ahead things began to shift.

Soul Revival before Spirit Revival

My wife was an artist, but her art had gotten lost in the shuffle of our ministry life. The Holy Spirit impressed on me that I should support her talent. We moved the furniture out of our living room and converted it into a studio. I purchased canvases and art supplies, and she and her girlfriends began to spend hours together painting for the first time in years.

I kept returning to buy more supplies from the art store, and the shopkeeper became interested in our story. He offered to let Winnie and her girlfriends host a show in his loft upstairs. It was not a real gallery, and it took some effort to convert the space into something that would work well. I went full tilt bringing in the right kind of lighting that would highlight the paintings and bring them to life. I did everything that I could to set the stage for my wife's success.

During our time in London, a Christian actor by the name of Nigel Goodwin had encouraged me in the Lord regularly, and we had become friends.[1] He was visiting the United States at the time, and happened to be nearby. As a special favor he came to Winnie's art show and did a dramatic theatrical reading for the crowd. Everyone was profoundly moved. We had prepared hors d'oeuvres and some of my musician friends were playing in the background. No stone was left unturned—I did everything that I could to help showcase my wife's talent in the best possible way. At the end of the day, Winnie and her friends each sold some of their artwork, and this brought major joy to my wife's soul.

It was now 1994, and I began to hear rumors of a fresh move of God. Several pastor friends called to tell me about extended revival meetings that were happening in Florida. They urged me to go check it out: "This is God; you don't want to miss this!" It took some time to rearrange my schedule and coax Winnie to come with me, but in January of 1995 we finally made the trip. It was now almost a decade since we had left Silverwind, and the Lord was about to close the chapter on that very difficult season in our lives.

We were surprised to find nine thousand people already seated in the sanctuary when we arrived for our first meeting. We never anticipated such a huge crowd for a Monday night service and had little to no idea what we were in for. Truth be told, I had to bribe Winnie to come to Florida with me, and I

1. Nigel helped start the Arts Centre Group in London, a worldwide ministry to Christian professionals in the arts and entertainment industry. For further information please see www.artscentregroup.org.uk.

was on pins and needles. This would be the first time in several years that we would attend a church service together as a couple. One of my pastor friends had saved us two seats toward the front, and I knew that my wife was not happy to be there.

As soon as the worship music began, God crashed in. His thick presence flooded the sanctuary, and everyone responded. The sheer energy of it reminded me of my visit to heaven as a brand-new believer. Thousands were rejoicing and many ended up on the floor laughing with joy. It was like a beehive. Winnie started to weep uncontrollably. She seemed oblivious to the fact that a man in our row had just jumped up as if he had been set on fire, doing wild sprints all around us.

Winnie sobbed throughout the rest of that service. Her mascara-stained tears streamed down her face, painting a two-lane highway down one cheek, and a three-lane highway down the other. She was overwhelmed by the nearness of the Lord and His tender lovingkindness. Later she told me, "Jesus came straight for me and welcomed me into His love embrace. He made me feel as if I was the only one in the entire room. I didn't even have time to prepare a repentance speech."

Something beautiful had happened with Winnie; she had been restored to her first love with Jesus. This was major! We went back for another meeting the next day. Personally, however, I could not figure out how to respond to the preacher who was inviting people to "take another drink." I could not see how "drinking" was an appropriate Christian message. Where is that in the Bible anyway? To my surprise, the preacher began presenting the words of Jesus from John 7:37: "If anyone is thirsty, let him come to Me and drink."

Although I had read the book of John hundreds of times, I had never noticed the word *drink* before. I had missed something that everyone else in the huge crowd all seemed to understand.

Their activity was foreign to me. I did not know how to respond, yet my wife was connecting in a very deep way.

We were all invited to a special time of ministry at the end of the week. The prayer line of close to four thousand people extended far outside the building. People began falling on the ground under the power of the Holy Ghost. I felt nothing—except that I felt like the only person left standing.

Just then a helicopter flew over us. Spotting thousands of bodies lying in the grass, the pilot radioed the authorities. Clearly, they thought that there was some sort of an emergency, maybe a gas leak or something. We heard the shrill sirens as fire trucks, police cars and ambulances began pulling into the parking lot, with all of their lights flashing.

I wanted to shout, "Officers, don't worry about these people lying on the grass, they are all fine. Take me instead, please! There must be something wrong with me because I can't feel a thing." While the ministry leaders sorted it out with the emergency response teams, my heart was sinking into deep personal frustration. I was, nevertheless, still very happy for Winnie.

Soon after, we took a trip up to Toronto, where Pastors John and Carol Arnott were hosting extended renewal meetings. They, too, were experiencing a massive outpouring of the Holy Spirit. What we saw blew us away. The large church auditorium was packed with people who travelled in from every nation, and they all came hungry for God. Just as we had witnessed in Florida, by the end of each service thousands of bodies were lying on the floor in the wake of God's power.

This was all a dream come true, sort of. Winnie was responding to this holy chaos with childlike trust. She was experiencing a flash flood of God's love and was coming back to life. I, on the other hand, felt unsettled by this unique style of revival because I could not seem to experience God like everyone else.

Again, I always seemed to be one of the few left standing whenever there was a time of prayer and ministry, and at one point I told the man who was praying for me, "None of this is working."

He replied, "Oh, yeah, it's working. You just can't tell."

In the end, I left Toronto disappointed. Once again, for as far as I could tell, it seemed as though nothing happened to me during the week-long series of revival meetings.

Working Hard to Receive

While my prayers for Winnie were finally being answered, I was discovering that something was wrong with me. Over the last several years without realizing it, I had become very serious, and unknowingly, joyless. While the laughter and other manifestations of the Holy Spirit did not bother me during these revival meetings, I grew offended by what I perceived to be the lack of seriousness in their faith. Everything they talked about seemed frivolous and silly to me.

During the revival meetings in Toronto, for instance, a woman went up onto the stage to share her story. She said that Jesus had come to her in a vision during which He placed her on a swing and began swinging her back and forth.

That was it for me. Full stop. Swinging her on a swing? In my world, Jesus was busy carrying the burden for all of the lost souls. How could He waste time playing on a swing? I completely missed the fact that this woman was burned out from years of serving in ministry. With this holy visitation, she was restored to her first love.

Somewhere along the way, I had disengaged from my childlike faith with Jesus and re-engaged with Him through a militant type of faith. I had become a very serious missionary for God.

It felt impossible to connect with what was going on during all these different revival meetings. I was expecting everyone to be as serious as I was—a burden-carrying Christian who was continually renewing my mind with the Word of God. Little did I realize, I had become joylessly steeped in my own efforts for Christ.

I was expecting a certain type of revival, the kind that came with a serious message that produced breakthrough, transformation and a harvest of souls. What I didn't factor in was that this expectation was blocking me from entering into what everyone else was receiving with joy from the Holy Spirit.

While I knew that my backslidden wife needed a fresh touch from the Lord, I did not know how badly I needed it, too. After all, I was the one who never stopped going to church, who kept reading the Bible every day and who continued going out to minister and preach the Gospel. She was the one who quit. I did not recognize that I had lost my childlike sensitivity to the Holy Spirit. All of my activities were camouflaging the fact that I had become dry and religious.

Back when I had first been saved, I spent full days, weeks and months feasting on the Word and experiencing the glorious presence of Jesus. He was so near and I was so filled with joy that, at times, I felt as if I might burst—it was impossible to contain everything that was effervescing inside my spirit. Not wanting to scare my neighbors, many nights I would drive around the city praising the Lord at the top of my lungs. Knowing that the noise from my old mail truck's broken muffler would drown me out, I was free to rejoice, sing, shake and shout because of the ecstasies of His presence.

What had happened?

Here I was, twenty years after my first encounter with Jesus, in an environment where the Holy Spirit was moving in glorious power and explosive corporate joy. Even though His joy was coming straight for me, it was coming for me in a package that I simply could not recognize. The bliss of His presence that I enjoyed so early in my walk with Him was now being received by the thousands while I stood by on the sidelines. The truth is, I wanted to be touched by God so badly, just like Winnie had been touched.

After we returned home, I saw that Winnie was experiencing the glory of God every day. She quit her job, and we began travelling and ministering together. I had no idea what to do other than bless people and watch as they were noticeably touched by the same fiery anointing that God was pouring out in this current revival. This was a total sign and wonder to me because I still felt unconnected to what God was doing.

Hearing about revival meetings being hosted by several pastor friends of mine, I figured that both Winnie and I should attend. I thought that I would be more relaxed in the company of friends.

On the final night, the preacher was finishing his sermon and fell to the ground intoxicated with the joy of the Holy Ghost. I gasped out loud because it was clear to me that he was down for the count. This would have been my last chance to have someone pray for me, and I could not believe this was happening. What was the Lord doing? The preacher's wife then picked up the microphone from her husband's hand. As she started speaking, her South African accent was impossible for my Bulgarian ears to comprehend. I listened desperately, for I knew that I had to be missing a principle or a key to unlock all of this.

As I strained to understand her, I became acutely aware of my extreme intensity level. I burst out laughing at myself. *Ha, ha, ha, this is so funny,* I thought. *I'm trying so incredibly hard, and I'm going for broke here, spending all of my time and money to travel everywhere and do whatever I can to try to get this anointing. What on earth am I doing? Oh, man, ha, ha, ha, ha, this is so funny!*

I had had a moment of clarity, and it had struck me as funny. But it was only funny for a minute, and now that minute was up. I wanted to stop laughing. My frustration was raw, but I continued to laugh.

Suddenly it hit me. What I had been waiting for all of these months was finally happening to me.

It took a solid nine months for me to catch what Winnie had received in a single moment—the pure bliss and ecstatic joy of Christ's embrace. The Holy Spirit was laughing inside me. He was using my own belly.

From my heart I cried out, "Lord, I don't want just to laugh a little bit; I want everything to change."

And that was the moment. I heard the Lord say, *I'm here to stay, Georgian.*

As He spoke those words, everything on the inside of me began to spin. I felt as if I were a blender, and He had pressed his thumb on my belly button for top speed—and it felt really good. The jet streams of the Holy Spirit blew right through my spirit, propelling me back up into the high altitudes of His grace. He began to take control of my life again. First I was laughing and then my arms started spinning.

I looked like a human windmill, but I did not mind one bit. God was freeing me from the pent-up emotions I held after so many years of struggles and disappointments.

Under the Influence of the Holy Spirit

Our marital problems and the various trials that we had experienced in life and ministry had all compounded one another. By unconsciously taking these struggles into my own hands, I had let go of my Helper's hand. Now the Lord was releasing me from a heavy sense of failure. With His grace, the Holy Spirit was disarming my efforts-based version of Christianity.

I had been taking a hard look at faith and the goodness of God in pursuing me ever since the trip to Bulgaria with Pastor John. But when I read Ephesians 2:8–9 again after this experience at the revival meeting, it clicked in my mind for the first time how faith works together with grace: "For it is by God's grace that you have been saved through faith. It is not the result of your own efforts, but God's gift, so that no one can boast about it" (Ephesians 2:8–9 GNT).

Strong's concordance defines *grace* as "the divine influence upon the heart, and its reflection in the life" (*Strong's* 5485). While grace is God's ability to persuade us, I like to say that it is His ability to "mess" with us and alter us in the most remarkable of ways. Only the Lord could mess with an old barren couple to make them the father and mother of many nations, or convert a bigot and religious terrorist into the apostle who taught the first-century Gentile world and laid down the spiritual foundation that we are still studying today.

The struggles in my marriage were over because He had gloriously overtaken both of us. The Lord revived Winnie first, which allowed her to build some speed with room to lift off. When I finally got touched months after her, I had to catch up so that we could run together. Oftentimes I would come home to find her on the floor laughing because God had touched her so deeply. Her long hair would be swishing across the floor, and I started to joke that we no longer needed a mop. The Lord had orchestrated everything. How I thank Him for His grace!

Out of the Ashes

Back when Winnie and I were praying about whether or not to leave Silverwind, the Lord had given her the Scripture about Abraham and Sarah to inspire us to step out where He was leading. In that verse, I now recognized the prophetic pattern and His supernatural grace operating in our lives.

From the text in Genesis 17, we can determine that it took about three months from the time that God appeared to Abram before his wife became pregnant with Isaac. At that point Abram and Sarai began to call each other by their new God-given names: Abraham, "father of many nations," and Sarah, "princess." They were speaking their new identities over each other, affirming God's plan for their lives.

Sarah had been barren her entire life, but the Lord waited until Abraham was a hundred years old before He resurrected her womb: "And Abraham's faith did not weaken, even though, at about 100 years of age, he figured his body was as good as dead—and so was Sarah's womb" (Romans 4:19 NLT). It took the power of the Holy Spirit to birth Isaac ("laughter") supernaturally.

Hebrews 11:11 describes this power that Sarah received in order to conceive: "By faith also Sarah, herself barren, received power for the conception of seed, even beyond the opportune age, since she considered the One having promised faithful" (Hebrews 11:11 BLB). The Greek word used for *power* in this verse is the same word for *power* describing the Holy Spirit outpouring on Pentecost in Acts 1:8. It is *dunamis* or *dynamis* (*Strong's* 1411) and means "power through God's ability." It forms words like *dynamite, dynamo* and *dynamic*.

When God poured out His power on the Day of Pentecost, one hundred and twenty disciples of Jesus in the Upper Room received the Holy Spirit, resulting in three thousand souls being added to the Church that very day. The supernatural Body of Christ has not stopped growing ever since.

Today, Winnie likes to testify, "That same power is the power that resurrected me from the dead." She explains that she was raised from the religious dead after being contaminated with MPS ("man-pleasing spirit"), a deadly virus that left her feeling like a failure and a hypocrite. Now she is no longer striving to please man; she is joyfully alive to God instead. Jesus graciously and beautifully returned my wife to her first-love passion, and she has been marked by joy and laughter ever since. She emerged from the ashes of discouragement and broken dreams and was transformed into a mighty woman of faith with a powerful teaching gift.

Beyond an answer to prayer, what God did for us far exceeded anything that I could have ever imagined or hoped for. We began praying and reading the Word together, and just like Abraham and Sarah, we started to speak to God's identity and destiny over each other.

Spiritually speaking, our marriage became a marriage of grace instead of works. Shortly after, upon reading the sixth chapter of Romans, Winnie received the same revelation that the Lord had given me right after we had left Silverwind—to reckon myself dead to sin and alive to God through Christ. Now she joined me in the joy and freedom of this wonderful revelation. Up until that point I could never seem to preach that message on my own. It was in me, in my loins so to speak, but it was not until Winnie believed it, too, that our joyful Isaac ministry was born—one that came about by grace.

Our years of religious striving were over. To this day, we rejoice together daily as a couple. Our mornings are spent sharing Bible passages with each other and celebrating each new discovery. Everything is fully wrapped up in Christ and His death, burial and resurrection.

Our marriage and our ministry have been restored, and the lifelong transformation is here to stay. Even though we have faced difficulties and trials, nothing has been able to sink us again. Since 1995, we have experienced the extraordinary greatness of God's grace:

> In our union with Christ Jesus he raised us up with him to rule with him in the heavenly world. He did this to demonstrate for all time to come the extraordinary greatness of his grace in the love he showed us in Christ Jesus.
>
> Ephesians 2:6–7 GNT

Grace upon Grace

Our former troubles can never compare with what the Spirit of grace did for Winnie and me. He set things marvelously right for us—far beyond what we ever dared to hope for or imagine.

You have seen how the Lord led me in my journey of grace. Looking back through that difficult period with 20/20 hindsight, it is clear to see how He nudged me to take a series of seemingly small and unrelated steps. While I could not see how the dots would eventually connect, in the end I discovered that embracing what God arranges is the very best thing one could ever do.

How freeing it is to know that His grace never ends! The Bible tells us that out of His fullness we receive grace upon grace (see John 1:16). Maybe you are experiencing something difficult. Be encouraged! God's grace—His wisdom, power and love—is rolling out for you like a river, the all-sufficient gift that brings us to Christ, keeps us in Christ and fixes everything.

7

The Sanctified Heart

Winnie had begun an exhaustive study of the book of Galatians. One morning after searching through her Bible dictionaries and lexicons, she asked me if I would read Galatians 2:20 to her in my native language. Opening my Bulgarian Bible, I began to translate it to her: "I have been co-crucified. . . ."

Winnie made me stop mid-sentence, and we went over it together word for word as I translated it into English from Bulgarian:

Съразпнах се с Христа, и <сега> вече, не аз живея, но Христос живее в мене; а животът, който сега живея в тялото, живея го с вярата, която е в Божия Син, Който ме възлюби и предаде Себе Си за мене.

I have been co-crucified with Christ, and [now] I no longer live, but Christ lives in me; the life which I now live in the body, I live it with the faith, which is in the Son of God, who beloved me and gave Himself for me.

Winnie was astounded that this little prefix *co-* did not appear anywhere in her collection of English Bibles. I was surprised, too, but for a different reason: I had never noticed it before. It had never registered in my mind because *co-* is an ancient prefix and is not common in my modern Bulgarian vernacular. It took Winnie's investigative tenacity to uncover it for both of us.

As it turns out, my Bulgarian Bible was right on point. Created during the ninth century by Cyril and Methodius, two apostles from neighboring Thessaloniki, our New Testament was translated directly from the original Greek text. This is where we find the prefix *co-*. To put this into perspective in terms of a historical timeline, our Bulgarian translation was written more than seven hundred years before the King James Version was translated.

The Power of Co-

Co-crucified? What did that mean? Going to *Strong's* concordance and *Thayer's Greek-English Lexicon*, Winnie and I began our investigation. This powerful little prefix *co-* is defined as a preposition denoting "the closest possible union, closer than other prepositions could ever express."[1] *Co-crucified* can be found in the original Greek for both Galatians 2:20, as rendered above, and Romans 6:6, which says, "Knowing this, that our old man is *crucified [co-crucified] with* him, that the body of sin might be destroyed, that henceforth we should not serve sin" (Romans 6:6 KJV, emphasis added).

Decades later, Winnie and I discussed at length the ancient Greek prefix with Dr. Brian Simmons, the lead translator of the Passion Translation. We were delighted that he kept Galatians 2:20 and Romans 6:6 true to the original Greek:

1. Greek, *co-* (*sun*), *Strong's* G4862.

My old identity has been co-crucified with Messiah and no longer lives; *for the nails of his cross crucified me with him.* And now the essence of this new life is no longer mine, for the Anointed One lives his life through me—*we live in union as one!* My new life is empowered by the faith of the Son of God who loves me so much that he gave himself for me, and dispenses his life into mine!

Galatians 2:20 TPT

Could it be any clearer that our former identity is now and forever deprived of its power? For we were co-crucified with him to dismantle the stronghold of sin within us, so that we would not continue to live one moment longer submitted to sin's power.

Romans 6:6 TPT

The discovery of this ancient prefix and its implications were huge. Let me explain. The union denoted by *co-* reveals not only what was done *for* us, but also *to* us in Christ Jesus, who included us with Him in His death: "And we know that our old being *has been put to death with Christ on his cross,*[2] in order that the power of the sinful self might be destroyed, so that we should no longer be the slaves of sin" (Romans 6:6 GNT, emphasis added).

Simply put, He did not die alone on the cross; we died with Him. By "we" I mean that our old being was put to death, or as the Jerusalem Bible indicates, "our former selves." Furthermore, when Christ was buried, He was not buried alone. According to Scripture we, too, were buried in the grave with Him: "In other words, when we were baptized *we went into the tomb*[3] with him and joined him in death, so that as Christ was raised from the dead by Father's glory, we too might live a new life" (Romans 6:4 JB, emphasis added).

2. Greek, *co-crucified* (*sun* and *stauroō*), *Strong's* G4957.
3. Greek, *co-buried* (*sun* and *thaptō*), *Strong's* G4916.

This means that our fallen Adamic nature was buried in the grave with Him, bringing a decisive end to our old identity. On the third day, when Christ was gloriously raised from the dead, we were also raised with Him: "And having been buried with Him in baptism, *you were raised with Him*[4] through your faith in the power of God, who raised Him from the dead" (Colossians 2:12 BSB, emphasis added).

And where were we raised? To be co-seated in the Spirit with Him in heavenly places: "For he raised us from the dead along with Christ and *seated us with him*[5] in the heavenly realms because we are united with Christ Jesus" (Ephesians 2:6 NLT, emphasis added).

The apostle Paul continues to use this incredible little prefix, revealing that we have also been made co-heirs with Christ, and, furthermore, we are inseparable co-workers with Him: "Now if we are children, then we are heirs—heirs of God and *co-heirs*[6] with Christ" (Romans 8:17 NIV, emphasis added); "For we are *co-workers*[7] in God's service; you are God's field, God's building" (1 Corinthians 3:9 NIV, emphasis added).

This little prefix was a corroborating witness[8] to what the Lord spoke to me when He visited me in 1985. That was when He told me to reckon myself (*already*) dead to sin and (*already*) alive to Him, on the sole basis of what He had done: "Likewise you also, reckon yourselves to be dead indeed to sin, but alive to God in Christ Jesus our Lord" (Romans 6:11 NKJV).

4. Greek, *co-raised* (*sun* and *egeiró*), *Strong's* G4891.
5. Greek, *co-seated* (*sun* and *kathizó*), *Strong's* G4776.
6. Greek, *co-heirs* (*sun* and *kléronomos*), *Strong's* G4789.
7. Greek, *co-workers* (*sun* and *ergon*), *Strong's* #G4904.
8. The Textus Receptus, from which the King James Bible was translated, and the Nestle Greek text, used to create the New International Version and many other modern translations, both corroborate this use of *co-*. *The Interlinear NIV Parallel New Testament in Greek and English* also provides corroborating evidence. One example of this use of *co-* is found in its interlinear section for Galatians 2:20, "With Christ I have been co-crucified."

In essence, Christianity is unlike any other religion in that not one single part of our redemption is brought about by our own efforts. Christ included us in His death, burial and resurrection. With our very first breath as a new babe in Christ, we find ourselves already seated with Him, cradled next to His heart. As born-again believers we are born into union with Christ our Savior right from the start.

What Jesus Does for Us and to Us

In the book of Romans, chapters 3, 4 and 5, the apostle Paul outlines what God did *for us* through the giving of His Son. By believing in Christ's sacrifice, we have been declared *not guilty*, legally acquitted from all charges against us: "Consequently, just as one trespass resulted in condemnation for all people, so also one righteous act resulted in justification and life for all people" (Romans 5:18 NIV).

Providing that we have accepted Jesus as our Lord and Savior, His blood washes us completely clean and makes us justified (*just-as-if-I'd* never sinned, and *just-as-if-I'd* lived a life of righteousness like Christ). We are joyfully headed for heaven. This is profound—astonishing Good News for which we can be daily grateful.

But guess what! There is even more Good News. We do not have to wait until we go to heaven; we can abide in His holy presence as joyful saints right here on earth. His finished work includes even more than the forgiveness and atonement that He provided *for us*.

In Romans chapter 6, Paul brings everything to an entirely new level as he explains that on the cross Jesus also did something *to us*. By including us in His death, Christ destroyed our sinfulness. Now that we are born again, the Holy Spirit can reside in us with the beauty of His holiness. In essence, the apostle Paul is describing two different sides of the same coin—*justification* (what Christ provided for us) and *sanctification* (what Christ did to us). Both are provided in redemption as a gift right from the start.

JUSTIFICATION	SANCTIFICATION
Romans 3, 4 and 5	Romans 6:11
God reckoned us "not guilty" on the basis of what Jesus did in His death *for us*.	God asks us to reckon ourselves dead to sin and alive to God in Christ Jesus on the basis of what He did *to us*.

God has already finished the work; our redemption is complete. Now He invites us to respond and join Him in the bliss of reckoning it so with Him: "Happy the man to whom *the Lord may not reckon sin*" (Romans 4:8 YLT, emphasis added); "Likewise *you also, reckon yourselves* to be dead indeed to sin, but alive to God in Christ Jesus our Lord" (Romans 6:11 NKJV, emphasis added).

While justification means that we have been declared *not guilty*, sanctification means that we have been *set apart for God and for His holy purposes*. Ultimately, human beings can neither justify nor sanctify themselves. Both justification and sanctification are pure gifts, found only in the person of Christ: "For by one offering he hath perfected forever them that are sanctified" (Hebrews 10:14 KJV).

Here is the basic difference between justification and sanctification in a nutshell. You can be justified and believe in God's plan of salvation, yet somehow find yourself still struggling along and doing your own thing while here on earth. Returning again to Abraham and Sarah's story, we see the prophetic parallel. God had already reckoned them as righteous because they believed His plan for their future. Instead of waiting, however, they took matters into their own hands, as if God needed help.

Justification through faith changes our status with God. Sanctification through faith, on the other hand, is activated by a change of our identity. It was not until the Lord changed their names and they began to call each other by their new identities, agreeing with what God said about them, that they spoke forth their destiny.[9] While Sarah was barren all along, God waited for Abraham's loins to die, too. In this way, neither Abraham nor Sarah could take any credit. Then and only then could He move in by His Spirit and quicken their mortal bodies. God touched them and they produced Isaac. This is a type of sanctification. Upon salvation the Lord touches us inwardly with His resurrection Spirit and we become His Isaac, the supernatural fruit of God: "But you, brothers and sisters, are children of the promise like Isaac" (Galatians 4:28 NET).

The new identity of every believer corresponds to Isaac in this sense, whose name means "laughter and rejoicing." That is why our spiritual nature is ultimately permeated with supernatural joy. Sarah said, "God has made me laugh, and all who hear will laugh with me" (Genesis 21:6 NKJV). In the James Moffatt Translation, this same verse says that "God has prepared laughter for me."

Wow, what a great reward for believing! Just like our spiritual father and mother in the faith, we, too, are invited to respond to His loving voice, knowing that He has prepared laughter for us in our own faith journeys: "And he is then also the father of the circumcised who not only are circumcised but who also follow in the footsteps of the faith that our father Abraham had before he was circumcised" (Romans 4:12 NIV).

9. Abraham and Sarah followed an axiom of faith when they paired their confession with believing, as seen in this verse: "If you confess with your mouth the Lord Jesus and believe in your heart that God has raised Him from the dead, you will be saved" (Romans 10:9 NKJV).

The Lord calls us beautiful and holy in His sight, and by echoing in agreement with Him, we can celebrate what He says with His belief in our hearts. We should not allow our own performance failures or delays to make us bitter or despondent, knowing that great reward is awaiting us as we follow the good Shepherd all of the days of our lives (see Psalm 23).

A Different Spirit

Let us move forward hundreds of years after Abraham and Sarah to the time when the Lord brought the Israelites out of slavery in Egypt. As a free nation, they were on their way to a land flowing with milk and honey, a marvelous picture of redemption.

Experts say the actual journey should have taken the children of Israel ten days between the Red Sea and the Jordan River. But let's cut them some slack. Given that they were about 2.4 million in number, travelling with children and animals, we would certainly understand if it took them a little longer to reach their new destination. Their journey to the land of Canaan, however, took them forty long years. And incredibly, Joshua and Caleb were the only two adults from that entire generation to set foot in the Promised Land. What happened?

While in the wilderness, Moses sent twelve leaders into Canaan to spy out the land. They were on a reconnaissance mission and were told to come back with some specifics. Were the people many or few, strong or weak? Were they living in cities that were unwalled or fortified? Was the land rich or poor? Were there any trees? Moses even asked for samples of the fruit they found growing there.

On their return, all of the spies gave their reports. "It is indeed a bountiful country—a land flowing with milk and honey" (Numbers 13:27 NLT); however, ten of the spies did not stop

112

there. They described terrifying giants living in fortified cities and warned the others: "If we try to take the land, we'll be crushed like grasshoppers under the feet of these giants. We don't stand a chance against them" (see Numbers 13:33).

When Joshua and Caleb heard these evil reports, they tore their garments. They saw everything that the other ten spies saw, but their report came from an entirely different viewpoint.

> They spoke to all the congregation of the children of Israel, saying: "The land we passed through to spy out is an exceedingly good land. If the LORD delights in us, then He will bring us into this land and give it to us, 'a land which flows with milk and honey.' Only do not rebel against the LORD, nor fear the people of the land, for they are our bread; their protection has departed from them, and the LORD is with us. Do not fear them."
>
> Numbers 14:7–9 NKJV

The Bible says that Joshua and Caleb were of a different spirit (see Numbers 14:24). Their report came from God's point of view. They did not focus on the giants in Canaan; instead their emphasis was on the delight of the Lord. They knew something that the ten other spies seemed to have forgotten: *Israel was sanctified; the Lord had set them apart as a nation unto Himself.* The land of Canaan had been promised to them, and yet Joshua and Caleb were the only ones who believed.

Forty years later, Joshua and Caleb's report was authenticated in Jericho by Rahab the harlot, who explained, "Ever since we heard about you and your God, our courage failed us. Everyone in this country has been melting in fear because of you" (see Joshua 2:11). In essence, she was asking, "What took you so long to get here?"

Having grown up loving God's presence and His Word, Joshua and Caleb had united their hearts in loyalty and trust with the new thing that God was doing. Because the others stubbornly refused to accept what God had promised, however, Joshua and Caleb had to wait forty years until that unbelieving generation died off in the wilderness.

We know three things about Joshua that set him apart from the rest of the people:

1. When Moses changed Joshua's name, Joshua received a new identity (see Numbers 13:16). *Joshua* means "the Lord is salvation." This is the same identity pattern that we saw with Abraham and Sarah.

2. Joshua was mentored in the Word of God. Moses rehearsed the book of the Law in his ears continually and even prophesied military victory—that the Lord would blot out the memory of the Amalekites, the first nation to attack the Israelites after the Exodus (see Exodus 17:14).

3. He was hungry for the presence of the Lord. Joshua remained in the tent where the Lord spoke to Moses even after Moses returned to camp (see Exodus 33:10–11).

The Lord's Delight in Us

This key phrase from Numbers 14:7–9 helps us understand why Joshua and Caleb were worlds apart from the rest: "If the LORD delights in us, then He will bring us into this land and give it to us." That rhetorical *if* was for the sake of the people. Joshua and Caleb were anchored in the Lord's delights, but they were now reminding the nation of Israel. In the wake of the evil reports from the ten other spies, that *if* was simulcast with the tearing of their clothing. Joshua and Caleb were reasoning and pleading with them to believe the truth. They could have said "if the Lord is for us" or "if the Lord is on our side," but they chose to say, "if the Lord delights in us."

The Old Testament type and shadow of sanctification does not arrive by sheer human effort or formula; it remains a matter of the heart. A heart that delights in the Lord is a heart that has received the revelation that the Lord delights in His people.

David, for instance, knew the personal favor of the Lord. We can see it clearly when he said, "He *liked* me to make me king" (1 Chronicles 28:4 KJV, emphasis added). Abraham and Sarah were advanced in age and well past their reproductive years. At this point in their lives they could have felt embarrassed to call each other "father of many nations" and "princess," yet, instead, they entered into the delight of the Lord. Before too long they conceived Isaac. "Is anything too hard or too wonderful for the Lord?" (Genesis 18:14 AMPC).

These Old Testament saints stepped by faith into the delight and pleasure of the Lord. They were aware of His favor and learned how to follow Him with affection and gratefulness. While the Lord called the entire nation of Israel, only Joshua and Caleb responded in honor to God's infinite superiority over those so-called giants. They believed God and embraced His plan to step forward into the joy and blessing of the Promised Land.

How inspiring to read about these two who withstood the pressure against the opinion of such a huge majority, even under threat of being stoned to death! While these two Old Testament saints had God with them, we New Testaments believers have Christ inside of us. How much more should we be listening to and voicing the will of the Spirit of God within us, who is saying, "Delight yourself in Me"? "Delight yourselves in God, yes, find your joy in him at all times. Have a reputation for gentleness, and never forget the nearness of your Lord" (Philippians 4:4–5 PHILLIPS).

Jesus did not die just to get us out of Egypt and let us wander aimlessly in the desert of unbelief; He gave His life for something far more. He paid the price to get inside us and personally lead us into the Promised Land.

By His grace He shows us our wonderful new identity in Him. What His grace provides, His faith empowers us to obtain with childlike trust. Now co-raised in Christ Jesus, we are invited to behold the new and obtain God's precious promises: "Therefore, if anyone is in Christ, he is a new creation; old things have passed away; behold, all things have become new" (2 Corinthians 5:17 NKJV).

It is not so much a process to change ourselves as it is calling ourselves by what He has already renamed us. That is the conquering of the Promised Land: It is the Holy Spirit invading us and leading us in triumph to fulfill all of His promises by embracing what He has already done for us: "Embracing what God does for you is the best thing you can do for him" (Romans 12:1 MSG).

This is what I mean by saying that He has given us the gift of a sanctified heart! A wonderful gift to us. He has basically given us a piece of His heart and is patiently waiting for us to discover all that we are in Him so we can fulfill His dreams here on the earth: "And such were some of you. But you were washed, you were sanctified, you were justified in the name of the Lord Jesus Christ and by the Spirit of our God" (1 Corinthians 6:11 ESV).

Sanctification Is a Gift

Just like justification, sanctification is received as a gift by grace alone, through faith alone and in Christ alone. It is imparted to us through abiding daily in Jesus and through our intimate relationship. It is a gift that grows and expands continuously. No longer stressed by the whip of performance or the yoke of legalism, we learn from Him how to live in the unforced rhythms of His grace: "It is because of God that you are in union with the Messiah Jesus, who for us has become wisdom from God, as well as our righteousness, sanctification, and redemption" (1 Corinthians 1:30 ISV).

While most theologians define *sanctification* as an ongoing process never fully achieved until we wake up one day in heaven, that is not how I see it. Instead, please consider my point of view. Since our sanctification was wrought entirely by God, our own performance has nothing to do with it. On the basis of His finished work, He offers to us the privilege of engaging in a direct intimate relationship with Him, the Holy One. Prior to that, we could only be guided under the tutorship of the Law. Now that we have been set apart in Christ, by faith we enjoy direct access to God as a Father, and His promises to us as His children.

While our cooperation is necessary, our part is to fix our love gaze on Him. He is the master at guiding and helping us to grow in His holiness, and what we "do" comes out of our love response to Him. Talk about Good News of great joy! Once I embraced this wonderful revelation, it brought me so much freedom. Instead of worrying about my perfect performance and everything that is wrong with me, now I am daily giving myself into the sanctifying hands of the lover of my soul. Some say that this is a process, but in my world, it is a love-trust relationship with my heavenly Dad.

Marriage and friendship are both good examples of what I am talking about here, for one grows continually in these relationships. The word *process* is not a fitting description here, for its meaning seems impersonal. It would be, for instance, the last word that I would ever choose to describe my relationship with my beautiful wife. Our relationship is not mechanical and impersonal; our relationship is based upon love and the trust that grows in our marriage union.

The apostle Paul uses marriage language when describing the finished works of the cross, with the keen intent that, as believers, we see our new identity. We are "married to Another" and now belong to Christ, our heavenly Bridegroom: "Therefore, my brethren, you also have become dead to the law through the body of Christ, that you may be married to another—to Him who was raised from the dead, that we should bear fruit to God" (Romans 7:4 NKJV).

The moment that a man and a woman are pronounced husband and wife on their wedding day, they are a married couple, right then and there, one hundred percent. No bride or groom would ever say, "We're almost married: It's going to be a gradual process."

In the same way, we do not get sanctified gradually either.

The day that the couple says "I do" is the same day that they say "Goodbye" to everyone else. A groom cannot slowly wean off his old girlfriends one at a time. Can you imagine him saying to his bride, "Honey, I love you and I want to marry you. But I have to confess to you that I have ten other girlfriends, and I can't get rid of them all at once. It will be a process, and it may take a while. But if you marry me, and with your emotional support, I am confident that I can get rid of at least one girlfriend per year. And in the process I'll become more and more faithful to you"?

Would anyone consider a marriage proposal like that? Of course not! You would kindly kick such a person to the curb and say, "Go process yourself with someone else!"

In this verse Paul gives a picture of sanctification: "For I am jealous for you with godly jealousy, because I promised you in marriage to one husband, to present you as a pure virgin to Christ" (2 Corinthians 11:2 NET). It means having been set apart for the one you love. Remember the words of the apostle Paul: We have been honorably married to "Another." We have been joined to Christ and He to us.

> No longer will you be called Forsaken, nor your land named Desolate; but you will be called Hephzibah, and your land Beulah; for the LORD will take delight in you, and your land will be His bride. . . . As a groom rejoices over his bride, so your God will rejoice over you.
>
> Isaiah 62:4–5 BSB[10]

According to Scripture, we are already married to the Resurrected One: "Even before the world was made, God had already chosen us to be his through our union with Christ, so that we would be holy and without fault before him. Because of his love . . ." (Ephesians 1:4 GNT).

That is our identity; we are not just dating and waiting. We have already said "I do" to Jesus, and we can produce fruit unto holiness—such as healing the sick, feeding the poor and leading the lost to Him. We are married to the happy Bridegroom; daily we can enjoy the love and joy of the Lord as He takes delight in His Bride.

Jesus' Prayer for Your Sanctification

Our Lord prayed with deep love for you and me before He left this world to return to the Father. Hear His sanctifying prayer:

10. Hebrew, *hephzibah*, "my delight is in her" (*Strong's* H2657); Hebrew, *beulah*, "to marry, rule over" (*Strong's* H1166).

Sanctify them through thy truth: thy word is truth. As thou
hast sent me into the world, even so have I also sent them into
the world. And for their sakes I sanctify myself, that they also
might be sanctified through the truth.

John 17:17–19 KJV

After hundreds of years, the King James Version remains
a powerful translation. Now I would like also to present this
beautiful prayer by our Lord from the Passion Translation. This
is Jesus' prayer for you!

"But now I am returning to you so Father,
I pray that they will experience
and enter into my joyous delight in you
so that it is fulfilled in them and overflows.
I have given them your message
and that is why the unbelieving world hates them.
For their allegiance is no longer to this world
because I am not of this world.
I am not asking that you remove them from the world,
but I ask that you guard their hearts from evil,
For they no longer belong to this world any more than
I do.

"Your Word is truth! So make them holy by the truth.
I have commissioned them to represent me
just as you commissioned me to represent you.
And now I dedicate myself to them as a holy sacrifice
so that they will live as fully dedicated to God
and be made holy by your truth."

John 17:13–19 TPT

8

God's Party for You

From the beginning, Winnie and I were soul winners at heart, and during my ministerial ordination I was commissioned to be an evangelist. When the music came to a close during our Silverwind concerts, it was my role to lead the crowd in an altar call. Our concerts were worshipful, and the Holy Spirit actively drew people's hearts. Seeing souls come to Christ was my favorite part of the night.

Now, as Winnie and I transitioned into our new season, the Lord began to enlarge our vision for what evangelism could look like. One day, I felt prompted to study Jesus' story of the Prodigal Son. As I re-read Luke 15, my attention shifted to the father instead of the younger son.

After asking for his inheritance, the younger son was in essence saying to his father, "I don't care what happens to you, whether you live or die, I just want to do my own thing."

The son took his inheritance and spent all of it on reckless living. When his last dime was gone, a severe famine spread throughout the country where he was living. He had nothing to eat and, by sheer desperation, took a job feeding pigs. Remembering that the workers at his father's estate always had full bellies, he determined to return home. Hoping that he would not be turned away, he rehearsed his repentance speech, which went something like this: "Father, I have sinned against you and against heaven. I am no longer fit to be called your son; would you please allow me to become a servant in your household?"

The father saw his son returning from a far-off distance and immediately had compassion for him. Instead of waiting, he raced to meet his son, seized him and embraced him: "When he was still a great way off, his father saw him and had compassion, and ran and fell on his neck and kissed him" (Luke 15:20 NKJV).

The son started to give his repentance speech, but the father cut him off mid-sentence. "No way! You're not going to be a servant; you are my son!" With that he summoned his servants quickly to slaughter the fattened calf and prepare a celebration filled with feasting and music, for his son "was dead but had come back to life."

The father's reaction was stunning. Instead of a stern rebuke, he restored him back into sonship through an embrace. He then clothed his son with a fine robe and shoes, put a family signet ring on his finger and spared no expense in celebrating his return.

It is interesting to me that he could see his son from afar. Had he kept a watchful eye out for him all of this time? He could have easily disowned the boy and made him pay for his wrongdoings. Instead he ran and *fell* on his neck to smother him with kisses.

This wording *fell on* also means "embraced." It is the same word used to describe the Holy Spirit falling on the people who responded to the Gospel in the book of Acts (see Acts 10:44 and

11:15).[1] By pouring out His Spirit, our heavenly Father sealed us in an embrace as His sons and daughters.

The Lord began to speak to me: *That's what I want you to do, Georgian, stir up the salvation party throughout the nations. Many sons and daughters will be coming home, and they are coming from a place of abuse and rejection. They don't realize that their Father is waiting for them with open arms. I want you to be a part of preparing the lavish celebration so that the prodigals are welcomed into My embrace. I want you to prepare the atmosphere with joy for the full restoration of those who don't know their sonship yet.*

I read the words of Scripture again:

"But the father said to his servants, 'Quick! Bring the best robe and put it on him. Put a ring on his finger and sandals on his feet. Bring the fattened calf and kill it. Let's have a feast and celebrate. For this son of mine was dead and is alive again; he was lost and is found.' So they began to celebrate."

Luke 15:22–24 NIV

Winnie and I began running to the lost just as the father ran to his son. This mandate from the Lord caused us to take on Global Celebration as our new name, and these verses shaped our ministry model. We began to embrace the harvest with joy by connecting with heaven's bliss over every new birth: "In the same way, I tell you, there is joy in the presence of the angels of God over one sinner who repents" (Luke 15:10).

Heaven is dripping with celebration over lost souls returning home. People all over the planet are getting saved in droves every day, and we need to stay connected to the extreme joy of that.

1. The Greek word used for "fell on" in Luke 15, Acts 10 and Acts 11 is *epepesen*, Strong's G1968.

"Fattened Calf" Celebrations

Today, as we travel to developing nations, our missionary crusades often look like community block parties. People come from miles around as they are welcomed with hugs, prayers for healing, feasting and celebration. As we preach the Gospel, it is astounding to see hearts respond to the lovingkindness of Jesus.

By divine providence, once our marriage was restored and Winnie and I began to minister together again, we began our first international effort in Kazanlak, Bulgaria. Known as the rose-oil capital of the world, this city is home to an impoverished community of thousands of Gypsies[2] who make up the primary labor force for the "Valley of Roses," handpicking rose buds.

During our Kazanlak ministry visits, we would always take the local Gypsy pastors and leaders out for a meal and fellowship. Yana pulled me to the side one day asking, "Dad, why don't you feed the whole neighborhood? They're all poor and hungry, too."

I could hear the Lord talking to me in that question. My mind was scrambling to figure out how I could possibly feed thousands, yet looking back into her sweet eyes, all I could do was say, "Sure."

And so, it began. Our first "fattened-calf" celebration occurred in my native country, and it was the kind of party that we thought the Prodigal Son's father might have thrown! We learned that the Gypsies' favorite meal is *corban*, a fatted sheep stew recipe well known in the region. We purchased a flock of

2. The Gypsies, also known as Roma, are an ethnic people group with their own language, flag and customs. The community of Gypsy families that we are in relationship with call themselves Gypsies, even though in some circles it is considered pejorative. Consequently, all of us at Global Celebration use the word *Gypsy* with a very deep love and affection in our hearts.

sheep and hired a shepherd to fatten them up for our summer return.

As the streets were lined with pots cooking over firewood, the village grandmas stirred the *corban* with all of their special spices. It was wild and crazy; smoke was everywhere and God's extravagance was on display. Our meal was followed by passionate praise music, celebration, preaching the Gospel, prayers and lots of joy. This tradition continues today. Every summer we feed between eight and ten thousand people during a two-day open-air Gospel crusade.

Working with Pastor Dimitar ("Mitko"), a powerful apostolic leader and cherished son in the Lord, we have witnessed regional transformation throughout the years in Kazanlak. While the Gypsies of Eastern Europe are among some of the most despised and rejected people groups in that region of the world, we have never met a people who love better than they do. There is a powerful revival going on among these "outcasts," whose response to the Gospel has been passionate and with abandon.

Originally, this notoriously dangerous neighborhood was filled with violence, crime, drugs and prostitution. The police were reluctant to enter for fear of being beaten up. At that time, there was only one Christian family living there, and that was Pastor Dimitar's family. Fast-forward two decades: The entire village has completely turned around. Jesus is worshiped openly in the center square every day, and the church is in full-blown revival. A good majority of the people have professed Christ, and the neighborhood is crime-free. Today the local police call upon the Kazanlak church leaders to come and restore the peace whenever problems arise in surrounding Roma neighborhoods.

What a turnaround!

When God Multiplied the Chicken

Our fattened-calf celebrations have travelled with us around the globe. While visiting our missionary friends Rolland and Heidi Baker in Mozambique to speak at some of their conferences and do some outreach ministry, I noticed that the people were eating rice and beans every day.

When Winnie and I learned that they have meat only at Christmas and Easter because of the expense, we went out and bought five hundred chickens, and the cooks fried them up that night. When you fry chicken in Africa, the aroma goes everywhere. The surrounding neighborhoods could smell our chicken cooking; everyone was dreaming of chicken that night.

We had prepared enough chicken for twelve hundred people, which would feed everyone attending the conference and our special guests of honor from the impoverished garbage-dump community. To our surprise, an additional twelve hundred people showed up the next day because they could smell the chicken cooking. We were not sure what to do; our crowd size had doubled! The cooks began frying some small sardines to try to accommodate the extra people, and we all considered cutting the chicken into smaller pieces to try to meet the demand.

The Lord had a much better plan instead: He multiplied our chicken. The people had come hungry for greasy, fried chicken, and that is what everyone had. While only 1,200 meals were prepared, there was enough to feed all 2,400 who came. Every single plate received a full portion. Winnie and I waited until the end just in case there was not enough to go around, but our plates were full, too. I have no idea who had the original chicken and who had the miracle chicken, but I can attest to the truth that God does not skimp when it comes to hosting a feast.

The Chicken Churches

We continued to visit Africa every year to work with Rolland and Heidi. Together we planned a week-long crusade in Malawi, which would include a chicken feast for thousands of people. In poverty-stricken Malawi, there was no place to buy the amount of chicken that we needed. By sheer determination, we located a South African pilot willing to bring us the five hundred frozen chickens that we had purchased in Johannesburg.

The pilot stuffed his small Cessna with our frozen chickens and flew up to meet us the following day. As we waited excitedly for his arrival, another full day passed without any word from him. When Rolland made an inquiry, he learned that the plane had been grounded in Beira, Mozambique. Rolland and another pastor named Surprise Sithole flew Rolland's little plane down to Beira, where they found our chickens sitting in an airport hangar in sweltering 103-degree heat. That chicken was on its third day without refrigeration, just sitting in a pile.

As it turns out, the pilot was grounded midflight by Mozambican air traffic officials for insufficient paperwork. They were threatening to confiscate his plane. He dropped the entire load of chickens onto the tarmac and made his getaway.

To everyone's astonishment, the chicken had not thawed. Nothing was ruined; the chickens were still frozen rock-solid! The Lord had miraculously kept them. Rolland and Surprise loaded the plane and flew back to Malawi. When they landed, there was frost on all of the plane's windows.

We were in the subtropics, where the climate is always hot, and this area had no electricity or refrigeration. The people had never seen anything frozen before. They were touching the frosty windows and poking at the frozen chicken with pure fascination. It was spectacular for them, especially the children.

The next day, we drove stakes into the ground, stretched some wire to make a crude grill and began barbecuing. Everyone had his fill of hot, juicy chicken.

By this time word had gotten out all over town about "the chicken crusade." Thousands came and gave their hearts to the Lord, for they were so moved by this kind, caring, generous God. At one point, Rolland and Heidi gave a special invitation for those called to be pastors. Hundreds responded, two hundred of whom graduated from the Iris Global school for pastors. They planted churches in their respective villages, and today they are known as "the chicken churches."

Amazingly, we heard back from the pilot, as he had a desire to serve the ministry. Even though he felt that he had failed at his mission, the Lord had something different to say about that. This man was in the advanced stages of AIDS when he offered to fly our chickens. He was not feeling good at all. On top of that he was divorced, and his heart was broken. He offered his service to Jesus anyway.

The day after he returned home from his flight, his ex-wife called him for the first time in three years. There was an immediate change in their relationship, and they got back together again. The second day after his return home, he noticed that he felt good and decided to go get an AIDS test. The AIDS test came back free and clear. The Lord healed him from that terrible disease during his frozen chicken mission flight.

God is extravagant. He is overflowing with immeasurable love, compassion and joy. He is filled with delight for His sons and daughters, and to this day we find ourselves in perpetual awe, for the Lord outdoes Himself from one salvation party to the next. There are so many prodigals, and they need to realize that God is waiting for them with joy. He has prepared a party, not a rebuke.

We should never underestimate the Lord's joy, for it is one of the essential elements in heaven's culture. God wants His sons and daughters birthed in joy, which comes through our corporate emphasis on the performance of His Son. Jesus embraced the shame and suffering of the cross fully so that He could offer new birth to fallen humanity. He was eager to redeem sons and daughters back into the family: "[Look] unto Jesus, the author and finisher of our faith, who for the joy that was set before Him endured the cross, despising the shame, and has sat down at the right hand of the throne of God" (Hebrews 12:2 NKJV).

When Jesus accomplished His mission on earth, the Father anointed Him with the oil of gladness, the costliest and highest reward: "You have loved righteousness and hated lawlessness; therefore God, Your God, has anointed You with the oil of gladness more than Your companions" (Hebrews 1:9 NKJV).

The oil of gladness flows out from the heart of the Father, who is well pleased with His Son and His redemptive accomplishments. This is what I believe is described in Psalm 16:11 when it says that at His right hand there are pleasures forevermore. The Son has so pleased the Father in every single way that the Father's joy exudes from the throne continuously. That is what I experienced when I was taken into heaven and saw the angels swirling around God's throne. They were vibrating from the ecstasy and pleasure found in His presence.

While Bible translations do their very best with earthly words to describe that ecstatic joy and bliss found in Him, my personal experience lets me know that there are not human words to express the extreme levels of joy found in heaven.

Along with joy, there are many rich components that are part and parcel of heaven's culture. Things like love, faith, purity, honor, patience, compassion, kindness. They all work together. If any one of these elements is missing, that is a flag:

Something is not right, and you cannot ignore it. Joy without love, for example, is a disaster. In the same way, faith without joy is exhausting.

Join the Celebration; Don't Fight It!

Winnie loves to minister to impoverished communities existing in garbage dumps all over the world. A few years ago she went with a small team to a garbage-dump community outside Tijuana, Mexico, which I will tell you about in chapter 10. As she stood on the mountain of trash sharing the love of Jesus with one of the trash pickers, he confided to her, "These words that you are speaking, they are beautiful. They come from your heart, and I feel them go straight into my heart. I love to hear about Jesus and want to know more. In times past, groups came here reading to us from pieces of paper about God, heaven and hell. They made me and my friends cry; we felt terrible about ourselves. Now, whenever we see them coming, we hide."

The spirit of religious bigotry, similar to the older brother, will point fingers and leave people feeling condemned and unable to measure up. Instead of joining the party, the older brother was bitter about it. I wonder where that spirit comes from? Certainly not from above. In contrast, Jesus points us to the father in the Prodigal's story who let himself become a spectacle racing to his son. By custom, running was forbidden for a Jewish elder. He ran to his son anyway.

Just as it was humiliating for the son to work with swine, I believe that picking through garbage is on the same level. Hearing those trash picker's words to my wife wrecks me. People with seemingly good intentions made an extra effort to travel to the dump, yet compassion and love were missing. They brought the wrong spirit with them and caused the community to cry and feel condemned.

I was in that dump, too, when He stooped down and found me. Growing up with rejection and insecurities stemming from the absence of my father and the cruelties of the Communist system, I did desperate and crazy things to escape my pain. Trying to survive, I rebelled with drugs and promiscuities, sinking myself deeper into that trash pile. When He miraculously saved me, He blanketed me with His presence as I cried and shook for hours. Afterward I ran to the Jesus People to let them know what had happened. As we worshiped together, I saw Christ's hands extend toward me, welcoming me into His arms.

Later as I read the story in Luke 15, the part where the father put the ring on the son's finger, I felt as if I had received a ring on my finger, too. I felt valued and knew that He would never leave me or forsake me. God befriended me, promising to stick closer than a brother. In time, as He nurtured me in His love, this friendship ring grew into a ring of sonship, and eventually a ring of authority, and in that authority I am able to give out rings to other sons and daughters.

Reading the story of the Prodigal Son today, I can understand why the older brother complained and reacted out of bitter resentment. Obviously he had never used his own ring of authority as a son and heir. Even though everything in the household was already his, he acted like a servant. Hearing about his brother's party made him angry, and he refused to go. When the father pleaded with him to join the celebration, he responded with rejection and hurt. Citing his perfect record as a dutiful son, he charged his complaint: "Why are you throwing good money down the drain with this party? You never had a party for me, and now you're slaughtering the fattened calf for the one who wasted the family's wealth on riotous living!"

The father said, "My son, you've been here with me, at my side every day. Everything that's mine has always been yours to enjoy. Your brother who was lost is back with us. I'm overjoyed, and you should be, too. It's only right to celebrate."

This older brother had full access to his father, whose love and provision were always available to him. Yet it does not seem as though he knew how to enjoy the blessings or joys of being his father's son. I wonder how many in the Body of Christ suffer because they do not know God as a loving Father.

We see the same spirit when the Pharisees got upset with Jesus for touching the untouchables and dining with tax collectors and sinners. They did not recognize God's grace or know Him as a loving Father. They knew the Law, but they didn't know His holy hugs.

After speaking with the Samaritan woman, another outcast, Jesus explained to the disciples, "My food is to do what the one who sent me wants me to do and to finish the work he has given me" (John 4:34 GWT). After the woman encountered the love of the Father through Jesus, she rushed to tell others. The people in the Samaritan village were ripe and ready to receive the Good News of the Kingdom. They listened and received, and Jesus was nourished and strengthened by the joy of fulfilling His Father's will: reaping the fruit of the harvest.

The Identity of Laughter

The Bible tells us in Psalm 2 that God sits in the heavens laughing at the futility of the enemy. As God changed Abraham and Sarah's names and identities, they stepped into their destinies and became happy parents to their miracle boy, Isaac.

Isaac, "laughter," was not just the name of a boy; it was also the nation of Israel's heritage. God's laughter reverberated throughout Abraham's progeny, through whom Christ the Messiah would be born. As we look at the history of Israel with all of its holidays and festivals, we can see that celebration and joy are a very big deal to the Lord.

While it is tempting to let life's challenges sink our joy meters low, we should never allow temporary stresses to distract us from our connection with the Overcomer inside us. Right in front of our enemies He sets a banquet table for us. This is the secret to our joyful victory: "For Christ is for us the Passover lamb, sacrificed for our deliverance. Let us then live life as if it was a continual festival, with not a taint of evil or wickedness left, but in the purity of sincerity and truth" (1 Corinthians 5:7–8 BARCLAY).

Just as the Lord commanded the nation of Israel to conduct feasts throughout the calendar year, He now invites us to celebrate with Him continually. Every day, take time to connect with His joy for the harvest. Keep serving Him with joy. God made us, saved us, and now invites us to join in the marvelous work He is doing. Stay in fellowship, co-labor with him, celebrate with Him while He's winning souls throughout the nations. Celebrate His work in us, through us and all around us.

As we partner with heaven and celebrate God's grace corporately, we will rock the world. God is not going bankrupt; we need to get involved in His extravagant celebrations and join the angels in praising the victories of our Father. He is constantly birthing new souls into His Kingdom.

Your Place in the Story

Where are you in this story? Are you like the servants in Luke 15, rocking the house with music and dancing while smoking up the place with barbecues? Or are you like the older brother? What are you projecting to the rest of the world?

Imagine with me, for just a moment, the interpretation of this Prodigal's story. What if the servants who helped the father throw the lavish celebration were actually sons who had wasted their inheritances, too? Consider with me; could it be that the father also welcomed them back home with a celebration? Could they now be serving their father out of sonship and affectionate joy?

I like to pause and think about these things. As co-heirs over everything, we should keep our focus on getting millions of proverbial robes, rings and fattened calves ready every day, and celebrating the compassion of our God, who is actively saving the world around us.

I truly believe that in the reformation that is fast upon us, heaven's exuberant joy will flow through the corporate Body. The essential element of celebration is being restored for the sake of restoring sons and daughters. Equally important, fathers and mothers will raise their children with that celebratory DNA. As more newborn souls are celebrated and raised with joy, together we will raise an Isaac generation. This is what all of creation groans for: the revealing of God's sons and daughters.

Even if you were not raised that way yourself, let the Holy Spirit infuse your spirit with His unspeakable joy. He longs to "re-raise" you in the joy of the Father's love. Remember, this is not just a human joy that we are talking about; it is the joy *of the Lord*, which is integral to our identity in Christ and comes through the daily enjoyment of connecting with Him.

9

Joy Is Not Dessert— It's a Weapon

Several years ago I was asked to be a guest speaker for a conference on the East Coast. During my morning session, freedom and joy exploded across the room and people began laughing under the influence of the Holy Spirit. As the next speaker started his session that afternoon, he began by saying, "The season of joy is over now. I'm taking you to the desert, and we're going to work on your character!"

During the break one of the younger leaders came to me and said, "Georgian, it was so good when you spoke this morning. The whole conference really needed that outpouring of God's joy. The speaker that followed after you told us to stop being joyful, and we felt as if we were being scolded. Joy and building character are both valid and godly pursuits, so now we're confused. Please help us understand. Did we do something wrong?"

I said, "No worries. You didn't do anything wrong. Be at peace—tonight I'm the final speaker of the conference. When I finish, there'll be no confusion."

That evening during my session, I tried to be as kind and gentle as possible because I did not want to offend the other speaker. Sharing about the fruit of the Spirit, I pointed out that the Scriptures place joy second on the list, right after love: "The fruit of the Spirit is love, joy, peace, longsuffering, kindness, goodness, faithfulness, gentleness, self-control. Against such there is no law" (Galatians 5:22–23 NKJV).

Who could ever say that there is seasonality in any of the fruit of the Spirit? Could we say, for instance, that the season of love is over? What is the alternative? Should we stop loving? Does God ever stop loving us? (see John 15:9). Can we say that the season of peace or kindness is over? Impossible, for it is His peace that guards our hearts and minds in Christ Jesus (see Philippians 4:7). Are there seasons for stepping outside of Christ and His Spirit? Unthinkable! How, then, can we suggest that the season of joy is over?

Somehow the Lord's joy has been undervalued, resisted and even deemed nonessential. Joy is not an optional add-on, like something from the dessert menu. Paul, however, exhorts us to rejoice in the Lord always. God's joy is, in fact, for every season, and it is especially for our hardest of times—that is exactly when we need His joy the most. Joy is His strength to endure (see Nehemiah 8:10).

Needless to say, that night's session ended with explosive joy. The people were set free to celebrate God's goodness and share in His joy with laughter and rejoicing. Oh, how He delights to refresh and strengthen His people! Joy is, after all, one third of the Kingdom: "For the kingdom of God is not meat and drink; but righteousness, and peace, and joy in the Holy Ghost" (Romans 14:17 KJV).

Announcing Great Joy

The birth of Jesus, the Savior of the world, was ushered in by a spectacular angelic announcement: "Do not be afraid; for behold, I bring you good news of a great joy which will come to all the people. For to you is born this day in the town of David a Savior, Who is Christ (the Messiah) the Lord!" (Luke 2:10–11 AMPC).

God in His infinite wisdom and love provided the ultimate solution for the fall of mankind. He sent us His Son, Jesus, who gave Himself to the cross as the sacrificial Lamb offered for our redemption. Anyone who believes in Christ is given a new heart and a joyful new identity as a born-again child of God.

This Good News of great joy continues to spread through His believers, although not without resistance. Each generation has the privilege of passing this Good News and great joy baton on to the next. The last book of the New Testament prepares us for the celebration of Christ's return on earth and His final conquest over His enemies: "Let us *rejoice and shout for joy* [exulting and triumphant]! Let us *celebrate* and ascribe to Him glory and honor, for the marriage of the Lamb [at last] has come, and His bride has prepared herself" (Revelation 19:7 AMPC, emphasis added).

King David prophesied that long-awaited Day of the Lord in a Messianic psalm. Christ, the stone that the builders rejected, has become the chief cornerstone. David exhorts us prophetically to celebrate with anticipation that great day when the Lord returns: "This is the day the LORD has made. We will *rejoice and be glad in it*" (Psalm 118:24 NLT, emphasis added).

Not a Human Joy

Let's look at what Jesus said about His joy: "I have told you these things, that My joy and delight may be in you, and that your joy and gladness may be of full measure and complete and overflowing" (John 15:11 AMPC).

Clearly, the source of the joy that Jesus is talking about is supernatural—it is not a human joy. He paid the highest price for you and me to have it. How then could we possibly say that His precious joy is nonessential?

Perhaps it is time to reconsider our stance on joy. If we say that joy is optional or not necessary, are we not reducing what God has provided through our relationship with Him? By picking and choosing or doing our own thing, are we in essence saying that we are in charge and have control over His work in our lives? That kind of thinking is a renegade illusion conjured up from that old, independent self-existence, something I wrote about earlier in this book.

Now, please hear me. None of this is being said to put false pressure on anyone. God's joy is so extremely valuable and vitally needed by every believer, I hope my words encourage you. If you lack joy in your life, my advice is to ask the Lord to help you. As you continue to read His Word and stay connected to the Holy Spirit, His joy will flow, for joy is found in His presence and comes through abiding in Him.

During my visit to the throne room, I discovered inexpressible joy. Just as the Bible says: In His presence there is fullness of joy, and in His right hand there are pleasures forevermore (see Psalm 16:11). Let me describe what that looks like firsthand for you. "Fullness of joy" means high-voltage, lightning-bolt joy that makes you want to wriggle out of your skin every single second from the extreme ecstasy and bliss of His presence!

Joy in a Philippian Jail Cell

I have always been deeply impacted by the story of the apostle Paul and Silas, the first Christian leaders to set foot in Greece, bringing the Gospel to Europe (see Acts 16).

A young slave woman with a fortune-telling spirit had been following Paul around as he shared the Gospel in Philippi. After a few days, Paul grew exasperated with that evil spirit and he cast it right out of her. Her owners were furious since they made a great deal of money from her fortune-telling. They dragged Paul and Silas before the city officials, who had them severely beaten and thrown in prison without a trial. They were bruised and bleeding. A Roman beating was not a slap on the hand; it was brutal. Paul and Silas were thrown into the dark inner dungeon with their feet bound in stocks.

At midnight, while they were praying and singing, the Spirit of the Lord fell on them, shaking the entire city.

I can understand groaning and moaning, but *singing*? They were in severe physical pain while locked up in stocks. How is that even possible? The resurrection power of the Holy Ghost was being infused into them, enabling them to sing their praises to Jesus—so much so that it caused a massive earthquake. The foundation of the prison was rocked, the doors were opened and their chains unfastened. As a result, the jailer and his family were saved. The first church of Europe, which began in Lydia's house, was now publicly established and growing through mighty signs and wonders.

This story of power evangelism has been instrumental in shaping my view on joy. The Lord has often used it to remind and encourage me to rejoice in difficult times, see His purposes break through and His joy come to me and my companions, no matter the trials or the storms.

Indestructible Heredity

As sons and daughters of God, we have His very own life and presence in us, and that includes joy. His presence and His joy are inseparable: "For you are the sons of God now; the live, permanent Word of the living God has given you his own indestructible heredity" (1 Peter 1:23 PHILLIPS).

We have received His "indestructible heredity." God's spiritual DNA has been transmitted to us. Joy is in our makeup, for it comes from our heavenly Father.

Look at the first-century Christians. Ancient Rome was the most powerful war machine that the world had ever seen. It conquered all of Europe, the Middle East and Northern Africa, yet all of Rome's military might could not crush a small community of believers in its own backyard. Why? Because they were followers of Jesus. He was their leader.

Paul, who established the Church in Rome in the authority of Christ, displayed the invincibility of God inside him:

> Five times I've received thirty-nine lashes from the Jewish leaders. Three times I experienced being beaten with rods. Once they stoned me. Three times I've been shipwrecked; for an entire night and a day I was adrift in the open sea. In my difficult travels I've faced many dangerous situations: perilous rivers, robbers, foreigners, and even my own people. I've survived deadly peril in the city, in the wilderness, with storms at sea, and with spies posing as believers. I've toiled to the point of exhaustion and gone through many sleepless nights. I've frequently been deprived of food and water, left hungry and shivering out in the cold, lacking proper clothing.
>
> 2 Corinthians 11:24–27 TPT

God used this kind of fierce leadership to establish the undefeatable Church of Jesus Christ in Rome. Paul's unflinching bravery set the spiritual tone for all of the believers who would not kneel to the Roman emperors or worship them as gods. This is why they were often executed out in the open. Spectators became converts as they witnessed the otherworldly glory upon them as they died. The anointing oil of gladness that God the Father poured onto His Son flowed down to His Body on earth, strengthening them with supernatural joy. By their enduring faith and indestructible heredity, Christians never bowed to the religion of Rome. Those emperors finally succumbed while Christianity expanded, for Christ in the believer is undefeatable.

Joy and Victory

In Paul's letter to the Philippian believers he said:

> I want to know Him inside and out. I want to experience the power of His resurrection and join in His suffering, shaped by His death, so that I may arrive safely at the resurrection from the dead. I'm not there yet, nor have I become perfect; but I am charging on to gain anything and everything the Anointed One, Jesus, has in store for me—and nothing will stand in my way because He has grabbed me and won't let me go.
>
> Philippians 3:10–12 VOICE

The presence of the crucified Savior makes us brave. His perfect love drives out fear, and His grace helps us to believe that we are more than conquerors. His fullness of joy gives us all the strength that we need to defy the threats of the enemy, and we rejoice knowing that nothing can ever snatch us from the Father's hand.

As we take a look at the faith superheroes in the Bible, we recognize that they were not necessarily large in stature but big in their revelation of who God is and His delight in them. They were completely enamored of the God of victory, the God of love, the God of joy. What else could make David the teenager face Goliath the giant with just a slingshot and a stone, and prevail? (see 1 Samuel 17:50).

Just look at Shadrach, Meshach and Abednego, who defied the wicked decree of King Nebuchadnezzar. Even at the threat of being burned alive, they refused to bow down to his idol: "The God we serve is able to save us, and He will rescue us. But even if He doesn't, we want you to know that we will not serve your gods or worship the image of gold that you have set up" (see Daniel 3:17–18). These three Hebrew boys were keenly aware of God's nature, character and supreme authority over all. After they were thrown into the fiery furnace, the king went into shock and awe. Not only were the boys fine, they were speaking with a fourth man in the fire—a clear picture of the pre-incarnate Christ.

Then there is Daniel, another radical worshiper, who prayed to God three times a day. When under threat of being fed alive to the lions, he praised God openly, not intimidated in the least by the wicked men plotting against him. When he was thrown into the lions' den, the Lord sent an angel to shut their mouths. No injury was found on Daniel even after a full night with those ferocious beasts.

Another one of my favorite stories is when the Lord told King Jehoshaphat, "Be not afraid or dismayed, for the battle is not yours; it's Mine" (see 2 Chronicles 20:15).

Surrounded by a coalition of enemies, Jehoshaphat went to battle with a choir of singers leading the way. As they worshiped, the Lord ambushed the enemy, who ended up self-destructing. It took Jehoshaphat's men three days to pick up all of the spoils, after which they returned with joy, for the Lord had made them rejoice over their enemies: "Then they returned, every man of

Judah and Jerusalem, Jehoshaphat leading them, to Jerusalem with joy, for the Lord had made them to rejoice over their enemies" (2 Chronicles 20:27 AMPC).

The Lord has promised to fight our battles; it is our job to take our positions and look unto Jesus. Our response to surrounding enemies, to threats and every intimidation that the enemy tries to throw at us, is to praise the One who promises always to deliver us and cause us to triumph. Joy is expressed in praise. As we praise Him, He fights for us. As we stay in praise, as we take our position in the finished work of the cross, the Lord will defeat our enemies.

While adversity in life is inevitable, it is what we do with those hard times and difficulties that determines how God can use us. That is why Paul said, "Don't ever limit your joy or fail to rejoice in the wonderful experience of knowing our Lord Jesus!" (Philippians 3:1 TPT).

As a young believer reading through my Bible, I was mentored by all of these faith superheroes. Each one of them was captivated by the living God. They were worshipers, intoxicated by the joy of His presence, finding strength to endure in every situation. Under His influence, they were made brave. Everything they did was for God, not themselves.

Our True Identity

A word of caution. In the book of Galatians, we see that there are two covenants, or two ways of being in relationship with God. They are represented by the births of Abraham's two sons—one by the slave woman and the other by the free woman (see Galatians 4:22–31).

Our true identity comes from the free woman, Sarah, who corresponds to the heavenly Jerusalem. The birth of Isaac, "the joy child," represents our joyful new creation. In Christ we are now the heirs of God's promises and blessings, fulfilling the prophetic word that everlasting joy shall crown our heads (see Isaiah 35:10).

In contrast, Hagar's child corresponds to the slave identity animated by the Law. As we take a close look at Romans 7:4–6, we see that we have *died to the Law*—in other words, when Christ died *He released us from the Law* and set us free to serve in a new and living way, a new Spirit-empowered life. This is the Good News of great joy! Now married to Him, we no longer bear fruit unto death, but fruit for life and holiness.

In short, the purpose of giving the Law to the Jews was not that they could fulfill it and thus please God by their own works. On the contrary, it was given to expose their utter inability to fulfill God's requirements on their own. The Law was designed to point to Christ, the Messiah. Romans 7:7–24 gives Paul's brilliant description of the out-and-out frustration of anyone with a legal mindset insisting on pleasing God by his or her own efforts.

That kind of struggle to fulfill the Law only makes one aware that without the power of Christ within, there is nothing but slavery to sin and ever-present evil. Now we see the inevitable conclusion to this fateful dilemma for anyone who is at the end of his or her religious rope: "O wretched man that I am! *Who will deliver me from this body of death? I thank God— through Jesus Christ our Lord!*" (Romans 7:24–25 NKJV, emphasis added).

When the Lord visited me in 1985 to abolish my man-made holiness program, He went straight to the point, asking me to reckon myself dead to sin. When I struggled to confess it, He explained that what I could not accomplish, for I could not keep the Law perfectly, weak as I was through my own efforts,

He accomplished by sending His Son in order to fulfill His requirements in me.

God went for the jugular when he sent his own Son. He didn't deal with the problem as something remote and unimportant. In his Son, Jesus, he personally took on the human condition, entered the disordered mess of struggling humanity in order to set it right once and for all. The law code, weakened as it always was by fractured human nature, could never have done that. The law always ended up being used as a Band-Aid on sin instead of a deep healing of it. And now what the law code asked for but we couldn't deliver is accomplished as we, instead of redoubling our own efforts, *simply embrace what the Spirit is doing in us.*

Romans 8:3–4 MSG, emphasis added

In the book of Galatians, the apostle Paul describes what happened to a group of thriving churches that he planted. In his absence they were visited by a group of Judaizers from Jerusalem. They were mixing the Law of Moses with the grace of Christ, thereby creating an unhealthy mutation, a perfect formula for bewitchment.

I often refer to them humorously as well-meaning "fathers-in-*Law*." Paul, however, had much harsher words to describe them and the danger that they posed to the young believers. As a result of their message of mixture, Paul said that those who were now trying to be justified by the Law had been "severed from Christ" and had "fallen from grace" (Galatians 5:4). It does not get much worse than that.

Fortunately for them, they had Paul as their father in the faith, who, as a labor of love, labored again until they were restored

145

in their union with Christ. Paul was able, continuing the parable, to cast out the bondwoman and her son from their midst:

> But what does the Scripture say? Cast out and send away the slave woman and her son, for never shall the son of the slave woman be heir and share the inheritance with the son of the free woman [see Genesis 21:10]. So, brethren, we [who are born again] are not children of a slave woman [the natural], but of the free [the supernatural].
>
> Galatians 4:30–31 AMPC

I am deeply inspired by the fatherly approach that Paul took, and I thank God for him. He gives us such a powerful example of how to protect our spiritual children from the bewitchment of today's "fathers-in-*Law*." This example empowers us as fathers and mothers in the faith to step into the authority given by Christ to block those trying to deceive and control the sons and daughters of God.

Seated in Heavenly Places

"Long before he laid down earth's foundations, he had us in mind, had settled on us as the focus of his love, to be made whole and holy by his love" (Ephesians 1:4 MSG). And how did He accomplish that? By His grace He raised us up with Christ and seated us in heavenly places with Him.

> But God, rich in mercy, for the great love he bore us, brought us to life with Christ even when we were dead in our sins; it is by his grace you are saved. And in union with Christ Jesus he raised us up and enthroned us with him in the heavenly realms.
>
> Ephesians 2:4–6 NEB

I am constantly challenged not to let these verses be truth that I only read, but an actual experience of the unspeakable joy and sweet communion in being enthroned with Him.

Admittedly, it is not easy to imagine that He has raised us in the spirit to this position, but the Word says it and so it is true. We must allow the Holy Spirit to open the eyes of our hearts to see from His perspective, for He rules from the heights of His throne with supreme authority over all things.

What pleasure He took in planning this! To snatch us out of the hands of the devil and the land of the dead was the costliest rescue operation possible—what a price He paid to have us in His presence! He not only rescued us but also co-seated us with Him in authority over the devil! There is nothing moderate about heaven; extreme love and joy are the norm. Just like the cross. What balance or moderation was there when our Savior hung naked on the cross? It took that kind of love in action to save us for the joy set ahead.

The enemy always wants to challenge us. In this life, circumstances may tempt us to feel rejected, depressed and never good enough, but that is just a memory of our old identity in fallen Adam. We now belong to the last Adam as joyful overcomers.

The joy of the Lord keeps us elevated so that we can see even the biggest obstacles from His perspective, just like Joshua and Caleb, who viewed the giants as insignificant grasshoppers in comparison to God's superior power.

Heaven is a wildly happy place, and God found a way to put heaven inside of our spirits here on earth. I always tell people that if you want to experience this joy, give it away. We have tested it, and it works, I promise you. There is so much of God's pleasure in carrying His love and joy to the hurting and the poor, and to the places where people have been dehumanized. There is nothing like seeing people get set free and healed. We have taken this heavenly joy to people living in garbage-dump communities, leper colonies, refugee camps and countries in conflict. Without fail, as we come with the holy hugs and affectionate kisses of our Father and Lord, people accept Jesus and are transformed.

You can try it, too, by taking it to any of the places around you where people are hurting and need the Lord. It could be where you go to work or where you go to school, or maybe your neighborhood. The Lord loves to pour out His heavenly presence. My wife and I like to call it "joy-fare." As the joy and presence of God come in like a flood, every stronghold of the enemy is disarmed.

Happy, Always Happy

Keeping in mind that the Word urges us to rejoice in the Lord always, I would like to share with you how that Scripture is uniquely translated in the Jerusalem Bible: "I want you to be happy, always happy in the Lord; I repeat, what I want is your happiness" (Philippians 4:4).

Who talks like that? Only loving parents who want their children happy. When moms and dads see tears or sad faces, they ask, "What's wrong?" Love desires their children's happiness. Sometimes when I teach about joy, I can sense some of the people thinking to themselves, *Yeah, sure, joy is okay, but I need something deep.* Well, I am here to tell you that joy *is* deep, and it is as deep as the heart of God.

When the apostle Paul wrote, "Rejoice in the Lord always," and then he repeated himself, "Again I say rejoice," he was emphasizing joy because it is not only essential, it is vital. The joy of the Lord is costly and profound, and that is the reason why Paul said it again.

My earliest mentor, Winkie Pratney, once shared with me that joy is the fourth most discussed topic in the Bible, right after God, man and salvation. C. S. Lewis said, "Joy is heaven's serious business." In all of my years ministering to the Body of Christ, I do not believe that we have taken heaven's joy seriously. But now that is changing.

Psalm 110 Generation

Early in my Christian journey, the Lord showed me this verse and a powerful vision of the future:

> The LORD said to my Lord, "Sit at My right hand, till I make Your enemies Your footstool." The LORD shall send the rod of Your strength out of Zion. Rule in the midst of Your enemies! Your people shall be volunteers in the day of Your power; in the beauties of holiness, from the womb of the morning, You have the dew of Your youth.
>
> Psalm 110:1–3 NKJV

What a beautiful description of how the Lord is planning to mobilize His army in the beauty of His holiness for the most powerful move of God on earth since the book of Acts. Dew comes just before the dawn.

This elicits special meaning for me as I spent some of my early summers in the Valley of Roses, a place I mentioned earlier. Fifty percent of the world's rose oil comes from there. Known as the "liquid gold" of Bulgaria, it takes more than one thousand petals to produce just one gram of rose oil. When the rose petals are full of early morning dew, they are hand-picked before the morning sun dries them, for it is the dew that holds the costly oil from the rose petals.

As a boy I had no idea that the Gypsies were the laborers who picked these roses. Yet, here I am today, connected with the largest Gypsy community in that area, and they are still picking these roses. They have accepted Christ and His finished work, and their entire community has been transformed. They call me Papa, and are my most joyful partners. Even in the midst of poverty they are living in exuberant joy. They have chased the spirit of crime right out of their neighborhoods.

The world may seem to be spinning out of control all around us, but, in actuality, the stage is being set for some of the most significant days in Church history. We are about to enter the greatest season of miracles, breakthroughs, soul-winning and transformation. Even when darkness seems as if it is about to overtake us, Psalm 110 reminds us that just like the sudden appearance of the dew before the dawn, Christ is pouring out His fresh oil of joy upon His people, which is His own beauty and attractiveness.

The book of Esther gives us an example of how God delivers His people. Chosen to be in the king's beauty contest, Esther gained favor in the palace. She went through twelve months of royal beauty treatments: six months with costly oils, and then another six months with special perfumes. What a beautiful Old Testament picture of the costliest oil of all, which was poured out on Christ after He accomplished His mission on earth: the oil of joy and gladness!

These beauty spa treatments were all in preparation for winning the heart of the king. In the end, the king was smitten with Esther's wisdom and beauty. He fell in love with her, married her and placed a royal crown on her to make her his queen (see Esther 2:17–18).

The Bible tells us that Esther was chosen by God *for such a time as this*. Her assignment was to save her nation from Haman's wicked plot to commit genocide against them. The Lord placed her at the right spot at just the right time. He had given her everything that she needed, and that included wisdom and support from her cousin Mordecai, who was always there to prompt and guide her.

Legal protocol would not allow her to approach the king without an invitation, yet the fate of her nation depended on her. The Jews spent three days praying and fasting before Esther made her move. She knew that she was facing death, but she also knew that she had the heart of the king. He held out his scepter at the sight of her and spared her life.

I find in this a picture of being seated in heavenly places with Christ, in whom we have the favor of God. We are allowed to whisper to the King. We have an audience with Him, and we can have confidence that He hears our prayers. This is the power of intercession. In the end, Esther asked the king for a new edict, and the Jews were miraculously spared from annihilation. Esther's delivery of God's people is still celebrated with great joy today during Purim.

The end-time billion-soul harvest will not happen without the extravagant joy that fuels the courage of everyday believers and gives them the divine strength to do the works of Jesus— "everyday believers" meaning not superheroes, but everyday people who are connected to Christ. He has ordered our steps to be at the right place and the right time; we are prepared to do good works as His bold witnesses: "I tell you the truth, *anyone* who believes in me will do the same works I have done, and even greater works, because I am going to be with the Father" (John 14:12 NLT, emphasis added).

I see this call especially on the young generation to do the "greater works." I see them dressed in the beauty of Christ's holiness for such a time as this, and anointed with the oil of joy and gladness, the costliest anointing oil.

There will be an acceleration in the last days, and everyone will be needed. I appeal today especially to the spiritual fathers and mothers in the Body of Christ, that we let the oil flow freely through us for the sake of the next generation. This is what is needed for the strength to accomplish the huge task ahead: "You prepare a table before me in the presence of my enemies; You anoint my head with oil; My cup runs over" (Psalm 23:5 NKJV).

For me, filling my cup comes from spending time in His presence and His Word, and celebrating His great works and power within us, no matter the circumstances. Let us step into the supernatural joy of Jesus.

I encourage all of my baby-boomer friends to stay in "joy shape"—the supernatural joy of the Lord will renew your youth. Caleb was able to swing his sword at age 85 with the same strength that he enjoyed at age 40 (see Joshua 14:10–11), and the Lord wants to do the same for you. Are you retired? He wants to re-employ you in His heavenly forces.

The Esthers need their Mordecais! Stay filled with His Spirit and mentor the next generation in His triumphant faith and wonder-working power. Here is the model with which Paul mentored the early Church in Rome: "Not that we have dominion over your faith, but are *helpers of your joy*: for by faith ye stand" (2 Corinthians 1:24 KJV, emphasis added).

Get Ready!

The Promised Land is ready; things will happen quickly. It will be just like Peter's experience. After he and his companions spent the night fishing without any results, once Jesus showed up, their catch was so huge that their boats nearly sank. The billion-soul harvest that is coming will be bigger and happen faster than we can imagine. It will be miraculous and will require us to stay filled with the oil of His joy.

Get ready to answer the call of "All hands on deck!" This prophecy of Amos is one of the most magnificent promises in the Bible, and I believe it is happening in our lifetime: "'The days are coming,' declares the LORD, 'when the reaper will be overtaken by the plowman and the planter by the one treading grapes. New wine will drip from the mountains and flow from all the hills'" (Amos 9:13 NIV).

10

Supernatural Joy and Justice

I will never forget the euphoria in the streets of Sofia, Bulgaria, when Communism fell. Scripture tells us, "When justice rules a nation, everyone is glad; when injustice rules, everyone groans" (Proverbs 29:2 CEV). Under their oppressive reign, our groans were silent for fear of being sent away to a labor camp. Because Communism fell so quickly, I gained an understanding of what happened in the book of Esther. As Haman was hanged on his own gallows and the death sentence against the Jews was reversed, the Bible says that the city of Susa exploded with joy (see Esther 8:15–17 MSG).

Justice has always been important to me because of the injustices that I experienced growing up in Communist Bulgaria, and I have learned that justice is very important to God. All throughout the Bible, the Lord sides with the victims of oppression and opposes those who carry out injustice. His laws support and protect the weak and vulnerable, and keep society safe from the terror of violent bullies and lawless criminals.

In this last chapter, I want to look at a very unique partnership between God's supernatural joy and His heart for justice. For "the exercise of justice is joy for the righteous, but is terror to the workers of iniquity" (Proverbs 21:15).

Justice for the Poor

Both the Old and New Testaments of the Bible are very clear about God's heart for the poor. Moses spoke this to the nation of Israel as he gave them God's commands: "There will always be some in the land who are poor. That is why I am commanding you to share freely with the poor and with other Israelites in need" (Deuteronomy 15:11 NLT). When the apostles commissioned Paul to go to the Gentiles, they emphasized that he "remember the poor," which, of course, Paul said he was eager to do (Galatians 2:10 NIV). The apostles wanted to transfer the God-given Jewish value of caring for the poor into the spreading of the Gospel.

I encourage you to feel God's heart for the poor and needy in these Scriptures:

> "If one of your fellow Israelites falls into poverty and cannot support himself, support him as you would a foreigner or a temporary resident and allow him to live with you. Do not charge interest or make a profit at his expense."
>
> Leviticus 25:35–36 NLT

> "At the end of every seventh year you must cancel the debts of everyone who owes you money. . . . There should be no poor among you, for the LORD your God will greatly bless you in the land he is giving you as a special possession. . . . Do not be hard-hearted or tightfisted toward them. Instead, be generous

and lend them whatever they need. . . . Give generously to the poor, not grudgingly, for the LORD your God will bless you in everything you do. There will always be some in the land who are poor. That is why I am commanding you to share freely with the poor and with other Israelites in need."

Deuteronomy 15:1, 4, 7–8, 10–11 NLT

These verses challenge us to consider the plight of the poor and let the Lord lead us in our response, both individually and corporately as the Church. In the following verses found in Leviticus, we can listen to the Holy Spirit and ask Him what these instructions could possibly look like today:

"When you harvest the crops of your land, do not harvest the grain along the edges of your fields, and do not pick up what the harvesters drop. It is the same with your grape crop—do not strip every last bunch of grapes from the vines, and do not pick up the grapes that fall to the ground. Leave them for the poor and the foreigners living among you. I am the LORD your God."

Leviticus 19:9–10 NLT

It is amazing to consider that God provides us with more than we need because He loves the poor and wants us, His children, to be able to step into the joy of His generosity. When we are cheerful givers like our Father, it produces gratitude and joyful choruses of praise and thanksgiving to Him. Look at 2 Corinthians 9:8–12 (NLT):

God will generously provide all you need. Then you will always have everything you need and plenty left over to share with others. As the Scriptures say, "They share freely and give generously to the poor. Their good deeds will be remembered forever."

For God is the one who provides seed for the farmer and then bread to eat. In the same way, he will provide and increase your resources and then produce a great harvest of generosity in you. Yes, you will be enriched in every way so that you can always be generous. And when we take your gifts to those who need them, they will thank God. So two good things will result from this ministry of giving—the needs of the believers in Jerusalem will be met, and they will joyfully express their thanks to God.

Paul wrote, "God loves (He takes pleasure in, prizes above other things, and is unwilling to abandon or to do without) a cheerful (joyous, 'prompt to do it') giver" (2 Corinthians 9:7 AMPC). The Passion Translation says, "Let giving flow from your heart, not from a sense of religious duty. Let it spring up freely from the joy of giving—all because God loves hilarious generosity!" God's heart is very clear. He does not begrudgingly execute justice. He is a radical and joyful giver to those in need. By helping the poor we bring glory and honor to His name: "If you oppress poor people, you insult the God who made them; but kindness shown to the poor is an act of worship" (Proverbs 14:31 GNT).

Justice for Orphans and Widows

The Gospel includes compassion and justice for orphans and widows in distress. These two segments of society lack two of the major roles God fulfills: Bridegroom and Father. The apostle James wrote, "Pure and genuine religion in the sight of God the Father means caring for orphans and widows in their distress" (James 1:27 NLT). Jesus wants us to be spiritual moms and dads for orphans and partners for widows—to care for them financially and minister to their emotional needs.

We are privileged to care for widows and at-risk children on three continents, and I would like to share one of our testimonies about a very beautiful group of children. In June 2012, after years of ministering in garbage-dump slums and a leper colony in India, Winnie and I became close friends with a local pastor who was also doing the same. We began working together with him to rescue abused and at-risk children out of the very slums where we were ministering. We began searching for a house for our kids, but no one would rent to us because they thought that our children would deface the property, disturb the neighbors and create a nuisance.

We prayed, "Lord, if starting an orphanage in India is Your will, then we know that You will provide."

Immediately afterward, we found the perfect building. It had been vacant for more than a year because the owner was unable to sell it. After one meeting with the homeowner, he agreed to rent to us and our children. We moved our children into this three-story house, affectionately named the Bliss House, and are so happy to watch our children thrive and grow. Whenever we look around the house at each of the rooms, it seems as though this building was constructed just for us. With its extra-large kitchen, a big laundry room and even several spacious bathrooms, it is truly one-of-a-kind. No families in the area build homes like this. We believe in our hearts that the Lord had our children in mind and prepared this house just for them!

We started out with twenty children and doubled that number in 2013. After four years, the landlord received an offer from a potential buyer on the house. He needed the money and wanted to accept the offer, but he graciously gave us a short window of time to counter the offer. Thanks be to God, we were inundated with a flood of support from many friends and partners, making it possible for us to purchase the house so quickly. Now our children are safe and secure in their permanent home! Today, they are excelling in school and dreaming hope-filled dreams. Isn't that just like our God? We are not just rescuing children from the abuses of poverty. He has provided everything needed to help us in the joy of raising future leaders who will change their world.

Freedom for Children

Winnie and I and our Global Celebration team have discovered an alarming trend. Some of the children in our care have come from various forms of child trafficking, and over the last decade we are witnessing an increase in those numbers. Vulnerable children around the world are being trafficked and sold as modern-day slaves.

In 2005 we met a man who runs a rescue operation in Southeast Asia and started to work with him. His primary focus is rescuing children who are taken from their families by drug cartels in Myanmar. The children are usually taken when they are only five or six years old, and then trained and used as soldiers to guard the drug and trafficking routes. Within a few years we were able to partner with our missionary friend, and take on the care of about 150 of these former child soldiers.

Ten years later this same missionary called us with the opportunity to rescue fifty children out of the hands of one of the insurgent rebel armies in the Philippines.

He negotiated a price, and we were able to raise enough money to obtain their release. We now care for two hundred former child soldiers in three countries in Southeast Asia. They are in safe hands, being educated and nurtured the way children should be loved in Christ-centered homes.

We personally visit them every year, and there are no words to describe how precious they are or the joy that fills our hearts to see them. Some of our favorite moments have been spent worshiping Jesus with them as they lift up their hearts in full devotion to their Savior. Experiencing the anointing and grace on former child soldiers as they sing to the Lord is extraordinary.

Love, Justice and Forgiveness

The Bible not only characterizes God as being a father for the orphan and a husband for the widow, but also a *judge* for the oppressed. Ultimate justice cannot be served apart from the God who provides justice for the afflicted and punishment for their oppressors.

Why is justice such a big deal to God? Because God the Father's loving answer for justice came at the expense of His Son, Jesus. When we see injustice, we want punishment. But when God sees injustice, He sees that Jesus was already punished on the cross—the ultimate injustice—to pay completely for the sins of both the victims and perpetrators and make a way for them to come to Him.

Several years ago, Winnie and I took a large team on a combined missionary trip and "Footsteps of Paul" tour. In addition to visiting sites and cities where the apostle Paul planted churches in Greece and Turkey, we went to neighboring Bulgaria for a week of ministry to several Gypsy communities. Travelling from city to city, Winnie and I would preach to the team during our bus ride. The end result? Holy Ghost laughter and rejoicing.

As we pulled into each Gypsy village, our team would roll out of the bus, fully drenched in the oil of joy and gladness. Our first steps out of the bus in that "condition" affected the atmosphere upon impact, and the freedom and joy were explosive.

Since so many Gypsy families are hungry for God, our arrival was like introducing coals of fire to gasoline. As we preached the glorious Gospel, worshiped and prayed for the sick, we saw many salvations and physical healings.

There was a young woman with us on this trip who did not appear very happy to be with our group. Most often, she sat alone in the back of the bus looking miserable. During one of our longer bus rides I walked down the aisle to where she was sitting alone. Her hoodie was pulled over her head, and her demeanor was withdrawn. She kept her headset on to listen to music and avoided eye contact with the rest of the team.

I asked if I could sit with her, and she mumbled a reluctant yes. With a few prodding questions I found out that she had never been around Christians like us, and while she believed in Jesus, she just could not understand what we were all about. She especially did not like all of our hugging; this trip was not what she had anticipated.

Wondering how she heard about this trip, I asked her how and why she came—after all, this was such a unique trip. She explained that the plight of the Gypsies had captured her. She read about how their fate under Hitler had in some ways paralleled the Jews during the Holocaust, and to this day, how unjustly they are still treated. The wall of prejudice that keeps them marginalized and living in extreme poverty in so many parts of the world broke her heart, and she wanted to be able to do something. She was looking for serious justice for this beautiful people group and began searching the internet. Once she found us online, she signed up to join us.

I let her know that we would do our best to make the rest of her time with us as comfortable as possible.

After visiting the famous ruins of ancient Ephesus, we spent our final night as a group in Istanbul, Turkey. We went to a restaurant with a semi-private room to have our goodbye dinner. While we were praising the Lord for everything He did during the trip, out of the corner of my eye I saw this woman fall to the ground and start shaking. The Lord was touching her. We quickly draped a coat over her and encouraged the rest of the team to leave her alone.

Eventually, she got up and came over to tell Winnie and me what happened. She had removed her headset on the bus long enough to hear me say that Jesus took our punishment on the cross for every sin, and that He paid the price for every crime ever committed. I was reading through these verses from Isaiah:

> Surely He has borne our griefs (sicknesses, weaknesses, and distresses) and carried our sorrows and pains [of punishment], yet we [ignorantly] considered Him stricken, smitten, and afflicted by God [as if with leprosy]. But He was wounded for our transgressions, He was bruised for our guilt and iniquities; the chastisement [needful to obtain] peace and well-being for us was upon Him, and with the stripes [that wounded] Him we are healed and made whole.
>
> Isaiah 53:4–5 AMPC

These words pierced her heart and impacted her all day long. That night as we worshiped, the Holy Spirit visited her powerfully. She went on to explain that two years prior, an acquaintance had sneaked a drug into her Coca-Cola when she was not looking. After she passed out, he took her to a hotel and raped her repeatedly throughout the night.

Now here we were in Istanbul on the two-year anniversary of that horrible attack. She had been bracing herself, fearing that she would not be able to handle it emotionally. She described her personal torment, saying that once the man entered her, it was as if he never left; the memory of him and what he did to her was a daily trauma and quite overwhelming. While she tried to forgive him, because he denied that it ever happened, forgiveness seemed elusive. It felt impossible to forgive someone who said it never happened.

That night the Holy Spirit showed her Jesus paying the price for that crime; there was an actual punishment for the violation against her. As the Holy Spirit ministered to her something happened. She cried as she explained, "That man is no longer inside me, Jesus the forgiver is. Jesus paid the price, and He brought His forgiveness inside of me. All of the trauma just lifted off of me, and I'm now free."

About two years later, this young lady came up to me during one of our conferences and asked, "Do you remember me?" As she reminded me of her story, I was in awe, for she looked so completely different that I did not recognize her. Her face was glowing, and her eyes were happy. She told me that she is a writer and just recently published her story. She was looking for justice for others, and Jesus helped her find it for herself! That night she gave her testimony to everyone at the conference, and there was not a dry eye in the entire sanctuary.

God executed justice for all sin through the unjust death of His Son. Jesus, the One who never sinned, became sin for us so that we could be made right with God (see 2 Corinthians 5:21). Through Jesus, the world can receive mercy and not punishment. To diminish the punishment that Jesus took upon Himself is to make His blood anemic or pink—taking away from its power to remove sin completely.

Some people do not see how *God's love* and *punishment for sin* can be compatible. In the same way that God is love, He is also completely just. God's love and His justice go hand in hand. The Bible says that God so loved the world (showing He is love) that He gave Jesus to be a sacrifice for our sins (showing He is just) so we could experience eternal life with Him (see John 3:16).

God's mercy and love do not cancel out His justness. God cares about every injustice, so He must punish every injustice. In order not to punish us eternally for our sins, He punished His Son so we could be completely forgiven of our sins. The punishment due us fell on Him when He was crucified on the cross (see Isaiah 53:5). Jesus did all He did for joy. The Bible says that because Jesus' heart "was focused on the joy of knowing that you would be his, he endured the agony of the cross and conquered its humiliation" (Hebrews 12:2 TPT). We are His joy!

If you have received Jesus as your Lord and Savior, you are a child of God (see John 1:12). The angels had a joyful celebration the day you came to Christ (see Luke 15:10). Instead of giving you the punishment for your sins, Jesus took your punishment, forgave your sins and gave you new life!

Some people feel that justice is when a person gets what he deserves. True justice in God's Kingdom is when Jesus receives the reward for what He paid for with His shed blood. Jesus paid for the salvation of every soul on earth. Injustice in the Kingdom of God is when people perish without receiving what He paid for.

The Joy of the Lord in Garbage Dumps

One of the best pairings of God's justice for the poor and His joy can be found in our unique ministry in garbage dumps all over the world.

Shortly after Winnie and I became engaged, Winnie led an Agape Force team of twenty young women from Texas to California, and across the border into Tijuana, Mexico. That initial trip to Tijuana planted a seed of compassion for those who live in garbage dumps, and, since then, everywhere we go around the world we look for garbage-dump communities. She has visited dumps in Vietnam, the Philippines, Cambodia, India, Thailand, El Salvador, Honduras, Mexico, Romania, Turkey and a big garbage dump in Nicaragua that we have visited every year for fifteen years. Garbage-dump communities are the epitome of poverty even though the people there work hard.

A few years ago, decades after her first visit, Winnie returned to the dump in Tijuana. This time she was strong, bold and ready to help the poorest of the poor—the ones who get no attention. After her trip I asked her how it went.

"Great," she said, "but I didn't like using plastic plates and plastic tableware. Next year, I want to bring china plates."

"Real plates?" I said. "How are you going to bring china plates for three hundred to four hundred people?"

The next year, she took sixty people with her to serve food. They caught Winnie's vision and brought china plates from home. Each person from the dump got to keep his or her plate. When they returned, I asked Winnie how it went.

"It was amazing," she said. "The china made the people feel special. But one thing I didn't like is that they had to eat on cardboard boxes. I think we need tables now."

"Are you serious? How are we going to bring tables from America for four hundred people? That is a crazy idea. You'd have to bring a whole restaurant."

"We're going to do it," she declared.

Ask and you shall receive! Friends from Southern California packed a travel trailer with folding tables and chairs. Not only did they bring tables, they brought tablecloths. And not just tablecloths, but candles and vases and fresh-cut flowers. It is crazy what the Body of Christ can do when you ask.

This time I went with Winnie and her team. We escorted our guests of honor to the tables, and then we all lined up to serve them. I brought my expensive violin and played my heart out. I was accompanied by a guitarist, and we sang specific songs to individuals once we learned their names.

After three hours of feasting and music, I sat down with a couple. The woman spoke a little English so I asked, "How long have you been married?"

She said, "We're not married; we've just been living together for six years."

I am not shy, so I asked them, "Why don't you get married?"

She looked at the man as if saying, "Talk to him about it."

So I said, "Hey, buddy. Obviously you love this woman. You've been with her for six years, so why don't you get married?"

He replied, "How do you start a family in a garbage dump?"

I said, "Well, you've already started a family . . . you live with this woman . . . so you might as well get married! Marriage is God's idea and is better than a casual arrangement. Get married. God can make miracles."

"Really?" he asked.

"Yes. God likes marriages—official marriages. Do you want to get married right now?"

They both looked at each other, smiling, and said yes.

"All right," I said. "I'm an ordained minister, and I'll marry you before God and before all these people."

Instantly, the white tablecloth became her wedding gown. A bouquet was made from the flowers on the table, and then two rings showed up. Somebody from New York had brought the rings without knowing why, and they fit. We had the rings, we led them to the Lord, and they made public vows to the Lord and to each other to be faithful. We took a big offering for them—the jar we passed around was stuffed with money—and we blessed them.

When we returned the following year, that couple was the first to see us from the top of the hill. We ran and hugged them, and they said, "Thank you so much for marrying us last year. Look, our lives have changed. With the offering, we bought a used truck, and we are starting a business."

We were all overwhelmed with happiness. We prayed for the couple—in particular for the man's dream of becoming a shrimp fisherman.

Then other unmarried couples came forward and asked us to marry them. Fifteen couples lined up—out of about five hundred people total. We had to grab white tablecloths again for wedding dresses. One of our team members was a professional makeup artist, and she had felt led to bring her professional makeup kit with her. It had made no sense to bring it to a garbage dump, but she brought it anyway. Sure enough, fifteen women needed to get their hair and makeup done and nails polished—the full beauty spa treatment. And we were able to do that.

We got the men ready and then performed a big wedding for all fifteen couples at the same time. After the wedding ceremony, the meal became a wedding feast. We led the couples to Jesus and arranged for people from the local team to give seminars on marriage and help them through the process of getting legal marriage certificates according to the local laws.

In 2017 we went again. This time our team brought wedding gowns, flower girl dresses and men's suits and tuxedos. Twelve couples decided to get married. A couple who had lived together for fifty years came forward. Someone brought a van that was equipped with mirrors and a dressing room for the brides. The women could go in, try on different dresses, look in the mirror, and choose the dress they wanted to be married in.

It was an astonishing celebration—even covered by the local TV news. The first couple who had married years before gave a testimony. We had a feast and music and dancing—and so much joy. Marriage has become a pillar in that community.

This glorious expression of love, joy and justice for the poor all came out of a seed of compassion God planted during Winnie's first trip to a garbage dump in Tijuana.

An Invitation to Do Your Part for Justice

I love Psalm 113, which is a song traditionally sung during Passover and one that Jesus and His disciples probably sang in the Upper Room on the night that He was betrayed. The next day Jesus was crucified on a cross outside the walls of the city where the garbage dump was. He picked up our garbage and lifted us up to heavenly places. Imagine Jesus singing these words, which perfectly express His heart for the poor and the needy:

> Who can be compared with the LORD our God, who is enthroned on high? He stoops to look down on heaven and on earth. He lifts the poor from the dust and the needy from the garbage dump. He sets them among princes, even the princes of His own people! He gives the childless woman a family, making her a happy mother.
>
> Psalm 113:5–9 NLT

The human heart without Jesus Christ is a rubbish heap—filthy and corrupt, filled with the stench of death. But when Christ comes in, He alters everything. It can take the rest of our days on this earth to try to comprehend this magnificent work He has done for us.

How does God lift the poor from the dust and the needy from the garbage dump? How will He put an end to child slavery and trafficking? Through you and me as we co-labor with Him.

Every nation has laws to prohibit the unthinkable practice of trafficking children. Even though these laws are in place, the systems of the world seem powerless to stem the tsunami of child trafficking. The inability to enforce good laws set up to protect minors from every form of abuse is a perfect picture of the religious individual described in Romans 7:7–24 who, while struggling to free himself by his own efforts, failed miserably. Paul describes this person as having been "sold as a slave to sin" (NIV). The phrase *sold as a slave* means "trafficked as merchandise" in the Greek.[3]

Do you see the problem? Only believers who have died to the power of the law and have been raised with Christ over the control of sin and evil (see Romans 7:4) have the authority to break the curse of the evil plague of child trafficking.

Government programs and nonprofit organizations do their best to help the poor and needy, and we are grateful for that. I, however, want to appeal to you and the entire Body of Christ to join this cause and put justice into action. Let's rise up with one voice and one heart and say, "Evil has to go! I will not allow it in my home, neighborhood, city and country."

The prophet Samuel was famous in Israel for the way God answered his prayers. The Bible says that "the LORD was with him and made come true everything that Samuel said" (1 Samuel 3:19 GNT). At this time in Israel's history, the Philistines regularly harassed and invaded Israel. The people cried out to Samuel asking him to plead with the Lord to save them because they knew God answered his prayers.

Samuel took a suckling lamb (a type of Christ) and sacrificed it as an offering to the Lord. The Bible says, "Just as Samuel

3. Greek, *pipraskō* (to traffic, that is, dispose of as merchandise or into slavery, literally or figuratively), *Strong's* G4097.

was sacrificing the burnt offering, the Philistines arrived to attack Israel." God answered swiftly as the smoke went up from the sacrifice. "The LORD spoke with a mighty voice of thunder from heaven that day, and the Philistines were thrown into such confusion that the Israelites defeated them" and drove them out, far beyond their borders (1 Samuel 7:10–11 NLT). The Lord kept their national boundaries supernaturally shut, and the enemy forces were unable to cross back into the territory of Israel. This divine protection continued throughout all the days of the prophet Samuel, King David and King Solomon.

We can see others in the Bible—small and great—who cried out to the Lord for justice, and He answered. Today we are the kings and priests of God made to reign in life through Christ Jesus. Jesus wants to rule and reign through us with peace and justice for the innocent, weak and vulnerable.

Together, as the Body of Christ with millions of believers in Jesus, I am calling us to use our God-given authority in heavenly places above the rulers of darkness in this world to declare the end of child trafficking. This includes rescuing children in current trouble and securing safe homes for them. Beyond that, the Lord is calling us to intensify our intercession in breaking the spirit of lust and sexual perversion off of the perpetrators, the pedophiles and the entire child pornography industry. We do not fight against flesh and blood, but against principalities and powers, who are under our authority.

I invite you to be a part of a justice cry heard around the world. Will you agree with me that this should stop? Will you cry out to God and pray, declare and raise your voice where you have influence—in your home and neighborhood, with your mayor, police chief and other governing leaders? God is the only one who can break the power of these enslaving addictions. In

Christ we have the authority to bridle them with our prayers. We have authority over these dark forces.

Recently I asked the Lord to give me His hope strategy for ending child trafficking so that I could focus my faith on victory in this world filled with injustice. He reminded me that just a few decades ago, cigarette smoking was allowed everywhere. On airplanes you had to walk through clouds of smoke to get to the bathroom at the back. Indoor smoking in public places slowly went away as society accepted the fact that smoking is not good for the smoker or those around the smoker. Someday that will happen with child trafficking. As we, the Body of Christ, shine heaven's spotlight on the evils of child slavery, society will reject this as unacceptable.

Oh, what a joy it will be in heaven and on earth when all children are free and this plague is stopped! By dreaming the dreams of God together, we will see the seemingly impossible become a reality: The global trafficking of children will come to an end in our lifetime.

Jesus Is Your Joy!

As I have talked of joy throughout this whole book, I hope it has been obvious that I am talking about the joy of Jesus Himself. He is a joyful King who was sustained through His suffering because He saw us, His Bride, His joy.

Joy is the oil of gladness that God poured on the Son as He accomplished His amazing mission. Read this prophetic psalm that speaks of Jesus: "You love justice and hate evil. Therefore God, your God, has anointed you, pouring out the oil of joy on you more than on anyone else" (Psalm 45:7 NLT).

The oil of gladness came from God. Jesus did not borrow it from the angels. Father God is the source of the oil, and He anointed His Son. That is the oil flowing down from the head of Jesus onto His Body, the Church. As this oil flows, so we hate evil, love justice, step daily into His pleasure and follow His guidance. The ultimate joy is fulfilling God's joy, which is to rescue every person on earth who is still in the arms of the enemy.

God wants to possess you with joy. He is inviting you to rejoice in Him and "always be full of joy in the Lord" (Philippians 4:4 NLT). This joy will sustain you, empower you, give you energy to finish your journey and then stand before Jesus someday to receive your reward—full of exceedingly great joy.

Continued from page 8.

Georgian Banov was born in Communist Bulgaria. As a teenager, he was a founding member of the first official rock-and-roll band in the country. He escaped the Iron Curtain and was mightily saved after coming to the United States. It was during the tail end of the Jesus movement in 1974 that he had a powerful encounter with Christ in Southern California. Soon after, he met Winnie, who later became his wife.

As part of the core team of songwriters, they helped write and produce the now-famous children's albums *Music Machine* and *Bullfrogs & Butterflies*, which sold more than 3.5 million copies worldwide, earning several Dove Awards and a Grammy nomination. Georgian also led the popular '80s band Silverwind.

In response to the Great Commission to disciple nations, Georgian and Winnie co-lead Global Celebration and travel extensively, holding apostolic renewal meetings and conferences worldwide. Boldly declaring the finished work of the cross, they bring joy and freedom everywhere that they go. Charged with a heart of compassion for the poorest of the poor, they also host lavish evangelistic feeding crusades throughout the developing world. Although the sounds and flavors of these international crusades vary from nation to nation, the river of God's extravagant love is always the same—deep, passionate, all-consuming and irresistible.

The Banovs are excited to be alive at a time when the Church will see the largest harvest of souls in history. Whether they are hosting Christian conferences, training students, hosting evangelistic feeding crusades, rescuing and caring for trafficked children or helping the homeless living in garbage dumps, their teaching and ministry are full of God's loving, joyful presence, bringing miracles and changing lives.

Georgian invites you to connect with him at www.global celebration.com or learn more about his school (for classes either online or in person) at www.gcssm.org.